Stories for Christian Initiation

Joseph J. Juknialis

Resource Publications, Inc.
San Jose, California

Editorial director: Kenneth Guentert
Managing editor: Elizabeth J. Asborno
Editorial assistant: Lisa Hernandez
Cover design and inside illustrator: Sr. Terri Davis
Cover production: Huey Lee

Reprint Department
Resource Publications, Inc.
160 E. Virginia Street #290
San Jose, CA 95112-5876

Library of Congress Cataloging in Publication Data
Juknialis, Joseph J.
   Stories for Christian initiation / Joseph J. Juknialis.
     p.   cm.
   ISBN 0-89390-235-7
   1. Meditations. 2. Christian literature, American. 3. Spiritual
exercises. I. Title.
BX2182.2.J84 1992
242—dc20   92-16485

96 95 94 93 92 | 5 4 3 2 1

*The following stories originally appeared in previous books by
Joseph J. Juknialis and have been adapted for use in this book:*
"Bread That Remembers" and "Chrysanthemums," from *A
Stillness without Shadows* © 1986 Resource Publications, Inc.;
"The Sitting Rock," from *When God Began in the Middle* © 1982
Resource Publications, Inc.

Contents

Introduction

Out of the Corner
of Your Eye: A Glimpse

THIS IS A BOOK OF STORIES. It was that before it
became anything else. And though you will find,
besides the stories, what some might call "other
scratchings," in the end that is all that is here, only
stories—the tales themselves, the stories of Jesus
and the stories told to him, your stories and my
stories, the stories of the Church—all stories. And
beyond that there is not much else—here or in life.

But back to where we began. This is a book of stories.
Some would say they are fiction. I should rather say
they are real, for the label of fiction enables all of us
to discount something too easily. The stories are of
life, and depending upon at which level you or I live
life, they will be more or less real for us. If there are
any you like—well, that may mean that somewhere

1

along the way you and I most likely spent some time in the same places. And if there are none which catch your fancy—that's okay too, for none of us walk identical lives and perhaps it only means that for one or both of us there is yet a home in which we have not yet shared a table or laid our head, and that means the future can be exciting. So read the stories, and let your heart fall where it may.

There are other stories here too—those called reflections. Because the reflections tend to be about what some folk see as "real" life, those folk would want to say that these are the real stories, but that would suggest that the others are not real or are less real, and then we would be back to where we began—which would do us no good whatsoever. So perhaps we could simply say that the reflections are only other ways of telling the first stories, for whoever said that there is only one way to tell a story? The reflections are intended to be just that— reflections—something to think about, daydream through, wonder about. Don't give in to the temptation to do anything else with them. While they probably have something to do with the original stories (or they would not be here), in the end they are what they are called—reflections, which simply means that they are meant to be sat with and not much else. Nevertheless, they are stories in their own right as well.

And then you will find here also the stories of Jesus. They are perhaps the most real, for every other story is little more than a retelling of his story in different times and places. So don't skip over his stories. It is because of his stories that all the other stories make sense. If it were not for his stories, then those who would prefer to insist that the first story in each section is not real—well, they would be right. And then those stories would be only fiction. But it is precisely because the Jesus stories are real that we are able to say all the other stories (yours, mine, and all the others) are real as well. So read the Jesus stories too and don't skip over them—or you and I might find ourselves living in an unreal world.

In this book, you'll find some invitations to tell your own stories, too. I've called those invitations questions. If you wish, you can tell the answers to yourself. And if you do, it may come to pass that someone will come upon you talking to yourself. Don't be embarrassed if they do. If they are real themselves, they will understand. And if they laugh or smile to themselves, well, it only means they have not yet come upon the real. So simply talk a little louder and perhaps they will be moved to tell you their own story, and then what is real will have become more recognized and known. The intended purpose of the questions, however, is for folk of your ilk to gather together and share your own stories. Remember, too, that your stories are shadows of the Jesus stories, and that makes them holy—which is no small thing. You can't get much more real than that.

Finally, you will find in this collection some rituals. They are for the most part the Church's story, and by that I mean the story of the faith community—not Rome's story or the institution's story or the official story. And since you and I are the faith community, the Church's story is in another way your story and my story and the Jesus story and pretty much most other stories as well. The rituals tend to tie into the RCIA process—that journey folks make who are in search of the real and call it faith. The Rite of Christian Initiation of Adults is people of faith and people seeking faith gathering together to name the real and discovering in the process that most of what people think is fiction is really real and most of what people think is real is really fiction. So if you think you may want to journey in search of the real, well maybe the rituals will help you find your way.

So that is what this book is about—stories. All real in one way or another. If you use this book, make sure it is fun for you. And if it is not fun, well then it may be that you simply need to give the book a toss, and that's okay.

You may notice that the order of the material following each story varies. For example, sometimes the suggested ritual precedes the questions, and sometimes the questions precede the rituals. It's only because at times one feeds into the other. Nevertheless, this is not a "how to" book, so do not read it too closely. If you find yourself using it as part of an RCIA process, do not use it like a teacher's manual. None of us ever liked school all that much anyway. Instead, use it like a notebook, which most of us used in school for doodling. So use these stories (if indeed you feel you must *use* them for something) to doodle with. And when you have finished doodling, you will find yourself with a picture of the real. Some folks call it God.

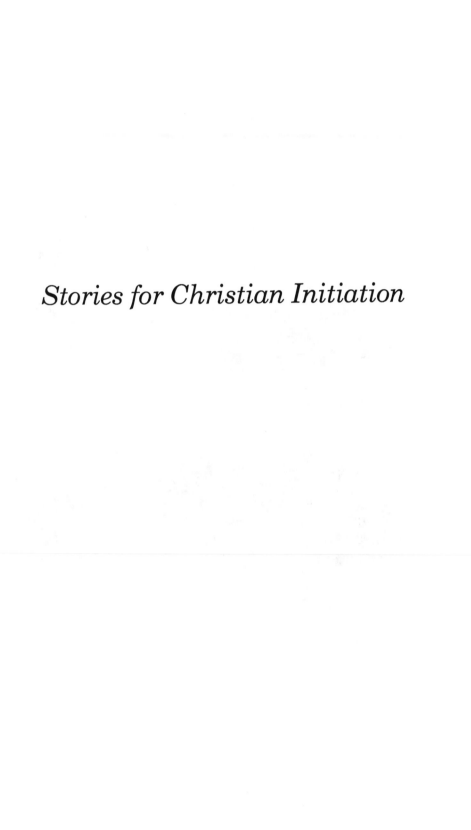

Stories for Christian Initiation

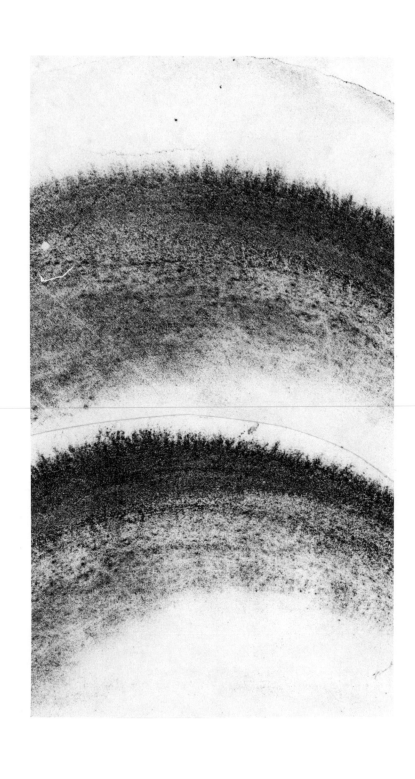

BREAD THAT
REMEMBERS

A LONG TIME AGO
people had not yet forgotten
that bread always remembers
what is spoken in its presence.
Then everyone knew that if goodness was spoken
among those gathered around the bread
then those who ate that bread would be blessed;
and if it was selfishness and evil that was spoken
why then those who ate the bread would be cursed
with cold hearts and hardened spirits.

There were in those days two brothers.
Many thought them to be twins
for they looked so much alike
not only in appearance
but also in what they did
and how they treated others.

However, though they were born in the same year,
they were not twins,
for the older had been born in January
and the younger in December
of that very same calendar.
Their mother had died in giving birth to the younger,
and so the two brothers
had been raised by their kind and loving father—
each reflecting his goodness and gentleness.
Perhaps that is why they were thought to be twins
by the many who knew them.

One day in early spring,
after they had grown to young manhood,
yet before either of them had married and left home,
their father grew seriously ill.
Before the seeds of that season had sprouted with life
the father died,
leaving his sons, then, to depend
upon their own goodness.

Together
the two brothers came before the judge of that land
so that the father's will might be unsealed
in order that each might receive
what the father had promised.
The reading of that will
revealed equal portions of life for each of the sons.
Because the father had loved them both,
without favoritism of any sort,

each of the sons received half of the farm
on which he had been raised.

At this, the elder son grew angry and resentful.
He had deserved the greater share, he insisted,
for he was the older of the two;
and with that he turned away from the judge
and from his brother
and left them both
alone
in that chamber of justice.

When the older brother arrived home
he sat in anger at the very table
where he and his brother together with their father
had shared meals
and love
and life.
There, at that table,
he allowed his anger to unravel more and more.
Shattering the gentle stillness
which had long been a family member,
he spewed curses and hatred
at the embarrassed and lonely silence.
Suddenly
he stood,
pounded the table with yet more violence,
and left.
In all of his anger
what the elder brother had never noticed
was the bread on the table.

Shortly thereafter the younger brother came home.
Having found the elder brother gone,
he sat and waited amid the stained silence.
When the older brother never returned
the younger brother ate his evening meal alone
in the torn darkness of that night.
There he ate the bread which had heard
the elder's anger,
the bread that remembered.
That night the heart of the younger brother
grew cold and hardened,
scarred with the same selfishness and hatred
which lived within the elder.

The next day's morning sun
was the sole source of light in the brothers' home.
The older brother did return
but without the gentleness
and love
which once were his.
So also did the younger brother live
without his father's gifts,
twinned again,
though now in hatred
as once they had been in goodness and peace.

During those weeks of summer,
the entire countryside came to recognize the change
which had come about between the two brothers.
Their hearts quietly wept in sadness
over that tragic occurrence.

There was in that village
a woman, both old as well as wise,
who had the knowledge not only of books but also
of hearts.
Somewhere in the middle of that summer
she invited
the inhabitants of the surrounding countryside
to a common meeting.
On a warm summer evening
all but the two brothers
came to the village square in the center of the town.
Men and women gathered;
children tagged along;
strangers were welcomed.

There, on the table in the center of their gathering,
was placed a single loaf of bread.
When it seemed that all had arrived,
the old woman who was known for her wisdom
came before them
and explained why she had called them together.
If is is true that the bread always remembers,
she said, then perhaps
we can bring blessings of gentleness and love
once again.
She then invited all those who had come
to tell stories of the goodness
which once lived in the hearts
of both the elder and the younger brothers,
and to tell those stories in the presence of the bread—
the bread that always remembers.

One by one, then, they came forward
and stood before the bread
and before their neighbors,
there to tell their own story
of how they had been blessed with life
by the two brothers.

Many stories were told that night,
all in the presence of the bread.
There were stories of how the two had once
taken in a stranger who was sick and lost,
and other stories
of the time a neighbor had broken a leg
at the beginning of the planting season
and how the brothers worked nights
by moon light
to plant his fields
after they had planted their own
in order that the neighbor
might have crops to harvest
come autumn.
Others told stories of how the brothers
had shared half of their own harvest with a neighbor
when his barn burned
and, with the barn, all of that season's labors as well.

All evening long villagers and countryfolk
stood in front of everyone
and, in the presence of that lone loaf of bread,
told stories of the gentleness and goodness
which once had made a home among the brothers.

When the last story had been told,
well past the time
when many of the children had fallen
asleep
in the arms of their parents,
all those who had gathered
made their way to their homes
and to the healing sleep which awaited them.

After all had left
the wise old woman who had gathered them all
stood alone at the table with the bread.
There, in the summer silence of that night,
she picked up the loaf of bread,
placed it in a sack,
and began her journey to the home of the two
brothers.
She arrived just before the sun,
when the nighttime had not yet begun to shed
her skin of darkness.
Her deed was simple
and quickly done—
to leave the bag which held the bread at the door
and depart.

As she made her way home
amid the early showers of morning sun,
she realized she was not tired
though she had not slept the entire night.
Instead, she felt within herself
a rising hope of life,

fed by the faint possibility
that perhaps the two brothers,
when they found the bread,
might just offer each other that bread
and with it
all of the goodness and gentleness and love
it remembered.

Reflection

Charlie Curran—not the moral theologian but the psychologist of Jesuit memory and blessedness—used to say in his psychology classes that it took him twenty years of being a professional counselor to realize that when someone came up to him and asked, "Father, could I talk to you for a few minutes?" what they were asking was if *they* could talk to *him* for a few minutes and *not* if *he* would talk to *them*. What they were seeking, he came to realize, was the very thing for which they were asking—they wanted someone to listen, not someone to talk.

We do need someone to whom we can tell our stories, for it is in the telling of our stories that we discover who we are, which may very well be the reason why teenagers spend so much time on the phone. It is the age when they are discovering a new self. How else to enter the discovery than by telling their story—again and again and again until they are sure they know it, until they are sure they recognize who they are, which may also be why some folks talk endlessly about themselves and their exploits—because they have not quite come to know who they are, and not to tell their stories would be to relegate themselves to oblivion.

Some would have us believe that the reason we keep telling the stories of Jesus over and over so frequently is so that we remember who Jesus is for us, and there is undoubtedly truth in that. Yet I would suspect an even more important reason is for us to remember who *we* are, for the gospels are really stories about us. It is not we who interpret the events of the Lord's life—despite the fact that we think we do. No, it is the Lord who interprets the events of our lives, and so it is that in telling his stories we are in reality telling our own stories and thereby discovering again (or perhaps for the first time) who we truly are.

The story of the Wedding Feast at Cana may very well be a tale of Jesus' compassion for a blushing groom whose feast had just turned to vinegar, but much more it is the story of our own lives and what happens to us when *we* run out of wine, when our futures, our hopes, the sources of our joy have all been drained to the dregs before the end of the party and we stand shamefaced before the world, empty-hearted and empty-spirited. It may then be that we discover God has created a new feast for us when life takes on new meaning in a way we never thought possible, when the unexpected turns the ordinary into something extraordinary, when the water does indeed become wine. Then the story of Cana has become our story.

Or the fact that Jesus knew well that foxes have their own lairs and that birds have their own nests but that he himself was without the space we all call home. More poignant, however, is recognizing those times when we find ourselves without a home and realizing that those have also been the very times we have been called to love, sometimes most deeply. The mid-life pregnancy which opens the doors of comfortable middle age to sleepness nights one more time. The neighbor who stops by for a casual chit-chat when what we had really hoped for was thirty minutes of peace and quiet before the family mob returns. The aging parent who takes not only the extra room but also all of the extra life. It is then that the story of Jesus' homelessness becomes ours as well.

Like the first grader who comes up to us bubbling with stories and seeming to have more of them than life itself, we too have spirits full of tales needing to be told if only someone will listen. And it may very well be that more of life happens in the telling of them than in the living of them.

Questions

- Share a moment from your life story—the best moment, the worst moment, or a moment you would like to live again.

- What is your faith story? How is it that you came to want to know about Jesus? How is it that you came to be a believer?

Resonating Scriptures

- John 6:46-51 (I am the bread of life)

- John 16:12-13 (The Spirit will guide you)

- John 21:24-25 (There is much more Jesus did)

Group Ritual

The suggested ritual and questions accompanying this story are appropriate for the **Period of Evangelization and Precatechumenate.** They invite participants to share their own life and faith stories with one another in preparation for deepening faith and formation in community.

In the center of the gathering is a loaf of bread. The story is told. Then all are invited to share their own stories of life and faith. After all have done so, a scripture may be shared and/or the Our Father prayed in common. The bread is then shared with one another, and in doing so, one another's journeys become the journeys of all. The path becomes one path lived together.

CHRYSANTHEMUMS

IN HER SEEDLING YEARS
she had heard those who were older
speak of God's word.
But when she asked what the word was
which God spoke long ago
their words would stumble and trip
as they tried to explain.
Still she kept asking,
hoping someone would tell her
what word it was
which God had once said.

One day
when she had asked her mother
one time more than she could endure,
her mother, out of exasperation,
finally agreed to tell her.

I think you are now old enough to know,
she explained,
as her eyes twinkled with a quiet smile.
The word God spoke long ago, she whispered,
was
chrysanthemums.

In awe she stood there before the revelation.
Chrysanthemums!
How powerful the word, she thought.
How special it sounded.
The very fact that it was difficult
for her to even say
convinced her of its truth
and its importance.
Chrysanthemums!

From that day on
whenever anyone spoke of God's word,
she
along with her voice
would jump up and down
and shout
Chrysanthemums!
Chrysanthemums!

In time she grew old enough for school
and when the new teacher asked
what anyone knew about God,
she volunteered her wisdom.
Chrysanthemums! of course.

At first the teacher smiled and paused
pleasantly startled,
his imagination captured.
After a while, however,
the teacher grew more adult
and serious
for answers need to be correct and proper
and tell of how life truly is.
Chrysanthemums was not the looked-for answer
she soon learned.

Thereafter she was cautious
of sharing her bit of divine wisdom.
Oh, on one or two occasions
she had suggested chrysanthemums,
but others still seemed startled
and unable to understand,
trapped between laughter and confusion.
Yet her mother would not have lied,
she reasoned.
The truth must be in
chrysanthemums.

Years later,
when her wisdom had aged
like wine
and seasoned memories,
she came to understand
why only to a few in her life
she had entrusted
chrysanthemums.

They were those whom she loved
and
who loved her
with gentleness and with strength
like a flower
with long-lasting faithfulness
and a common beauty
which survived the common.

Often she had daydreamed
why God would have spoken
chrysanthemums.
Why not a rose
or an eagle
or fire
or wind
or woman
or man?
Why chrysanthemums?
Truth, however,
is not always borne
with reasons—
more often with the heart.
And so she simply lived with her word,
absorbed its beauty
and became that word
enfleshed.

When she grew ill one final time
and memories gave the only strength that mattered,
she lay waiting

in silent peace.
A friend came, then,
one who had known her heart
and her dreams.
The friend brought her flowers,
chrysanthemums.
With the flowers placed
there on the table beside her bed,
she simply smiled in thanksgiving
and quietly closed her eyes.

When next she saw again,
she found herself in God's presence
and this time God smiled
and said
Chrysanthemums!

Reflection

Strange as it may seem, God does not talk God-talk,
which is to say that God does not speak religious
language—at least not any better or any more than
any other language and probably less. It is people
who talk in God-speak—theologians, preachers,
religious educators, parents, most all of us at some
time or another I would guess. And we talk it as if it
were God's language—except that it isn't. God talks
in human language. Our tongue. People-speak. Or
any other way you would like to say it. God does not
use words like *evangelization* or *trinity* or *salvation*
or *transubstantiation* or *grace* or any other such
churchy words. God uses words like *rainbow* or
telephone or *grass* or *camera* or even *chrysanthemum*.
It is we humans who have developed a specific
religious vocabulary to speak about God while God
speaks to us all the time using the stuff of human
life. It may just be that that is why most of us don't
think God is doing much talking, which is another
way of saying that we listen with the wrong set of
ears.

Sometimes, when I'm asked to lead an adult
gathering in some sort of faith reflection, I invite
those folks to make a list of where they bumped into
God in the last twenty-four hours. They usually (and
quite easily) come up with an impressive and
touching list. A stranger who stopped to help change
a tire. A teenager who cut their grass for free. At the
family breakfast table that morning. A walk in the
woods. A doctor's gentleness. A friend's newborn
baby. A letter. A phone call. A smile. An apology. A
touch. A summer breeze. And on and on and on. And
those same folks have no difficulty in interpreting the

events—which almost invariably becomes translated as *love*. So maybe God has a limited vocabulary of only one word, or maybe God in her wisdom figures there is no need to say any more. Whatever the case, I have come to believe that God speaks more outside of our churches than inside, simply because God is speaking all of the time—the glory of it all.

But no one can prove that, you may object. That is simply one more opinion, one more perspective, one more voice in a chorus of cacophony. But of course, that is the harmony of faith, the difference between a believer's ear and all other listeners.

God spoke once and life happened and that word keeps ringing in human ears through all of creation's lifetime. And that is why perhaps not everyone thinks s/he hears it or why all of us are not aware that God is always speaking—because it sounds too much like ordinary chatter. It sounds like the cries of those who are dying and the gasps of those being born, like heavy metal and country western and soft rock ballads, like teenage voices cracking with independence and hustlers pitching for a fast buck, like breezes as well as tornadoes, expressway traffic and shuffling old age, tears streaming with joy and also with sorrow. Such is the voice of God babbling away in incoherent baby talk yet able to be understood by every doting mother and father and person of faith.

Questions

- If you were God and could speak only one word, what would that be? (Be creative—make it something concrete, not abstract.)

- Make a list of major events in your life and interpret them in light of faith and God speaking. Share one or two.

Resonating Scriptures

- Genesis 1:1-5 (God spoke and creation happened)

- Isaiah 55:10-11 (God's word does not fail)

- John 1:1-5, 14 (The Word became flesh)

Group Ritual

Like the ritual for "Bread that Remembers," this
ritual is also appropriate for the **Period of
Evangelization and Precatechumenate.** It
focuses upon the richness of creation as a revelation
of God and an entrance into our experience of God.

Since God does indeed speak through all of God's
creation, assemble a varying array of objects—for
example, a rock, an apple, a bowl of water, a lit
candle, a stuffed animal, a flower, a feather, bread, a
sea shell, a piece of wood or small branch, sand, a
leaf, wine, some paper stars, whatever else may come
to mind. Arrange them as the central focus for the
gathering. Tell the story "Chrysanthemums". Reflect
on the first question from above. Read the story of
creation—Genesis 1:1-2:4. Invite those gathered to
reflect and share what they think God may be saying
about Godself in each of the objects present. For
example, a rock may speak of God's strength or of
God's permanency; a feather, of God's gentleness or
of God's ability to "go with the flow." Close with a
song or shared prayer.

A MATTER OF THE HEART

IT WAS AUTUMN
and it was raining.
And though it was a warm autumn shower
the dwarf ducked under the bridge
and into the dry slip wedged between the rain.

Now it happened that the troll lived there,
under that bridge,
so after the dwarf had brushed his coat
and shaken his cap free of the rain,
the troll said, "Welcome."

"Oh, I'm sorry," replied the dwarf.
"I didn't know this was your home.
I'll leave at once."

But the troll only held up his hand
and waved it back and forth

as if to dust the dwarf's thinking
clear of such intents.
"No need, no need to leave.
Please stay
and share with me this gift of autumn rain."

"Very well," said the dwarf.
"You are most kind.
It is a gift, indeed,
this autumn rain,
for autumn showers bring snow flowers."

"I beg your pardon?" asked the troll.
"What was that you said just now?"

"I said," repeated the dwarf,
"that the autumn rain is indeed a gift..."

"Yes, yes, but then after that?"

"That autumn showers bring snow flowers."

"Oh, you must mean
that April showers bring May flowers,"
corrected the troll.
"That is the saying, I believe."

"No...," replied the dwarf.

"Then, perhaps,
that autumn flowers bring snow showers,
for such would seem more true," insisted the troll.

The dwarf paused
and thought behind his gaze
before he spoke.
"No.
I said what I meant
and meant what I said,
that autumn showers bring snow flowers."

"But that cannot be," insisted the troll.
"I don't understand.
I have never seen snow flowers."

"That is because they are invisible,"
explained the dwarf.

"But if they are invisible,"
the troll continued to seek an explanation,
"how do you know they exist?"

By now
the dwarf was beginning to grow a bit impatient
with the troll
and with the troll's questions.
"They can be smelled, of course.
How else would anyone know they were blooming?"
To the dwarf it all seemed so simple.

"Tell me then," asked the troll with a smile,
now more out of disbelief
than out of interest,
"how do snow flowers smell?"

"Why fresh, of course," explained the dwarf,
"and crisp
and brisk
and clear.
They smell very much alive."

The troll simply shook his head.
"It sounds to me
that what you describe
is more a cold and wintry day
than the snow flowers you propose.
It's all too silly to be true."

"Believe what you will," answered the dwarf,
"but I know them to be
the autumn rain's gift each year,
blossoming with the cold
blooming in the frigid air
then disappearing in the warmth."

"Aha!" shouted the troll,
thinking the dwarf
had tripped himself up in the explanation.
"Tell me, now.
How does that which is invisible
disappear?"

The dwarf, however, saw no problem.
"It is simple, of course.
Once the snow flowers have withered
and disappeared,
their crisp, brisk fragrance

can no longer be smelled."
To the dwarf it was a simple matter of fact.

"Ridiculous," insisted the troll,
fearful of appearing the fool.
"You have simply given a new name
to what everyone already knows
as the fresh, clean smell of winter."

"But of course, my troll,
that is how it is with matters of the heart."

"Say that again, please," requested the troll.

"But of course."
The dwarf was most obliging.
"That is how it is with matters of the heart."

The troll smiled.
"Then you agree.
What you have been referring to
as the delightful winter fragrance of snow flowers
is in truth
the fresh clean smell of winter."

"On the contrary," insisted the dwarf.
"What you have been referring to
as the fresh clean smell of winter
is in truth
the delightful winter fragrance of snow flowers."

"Words, words. Nothing more," demanded the troll.

"I'm sorry," replied the dwarf.
"I disagree.
It is much more.
It is a matter of the heart,
and that is all the difference."

But the troll would not be silenced.
"I should rather say
it is a matter of reality.
I ask you, Mr. Dwarf,
you may speak of snow flowers
and fragrances
and matters of the heart,
but
where does reality lie?
What is the real?
That is the question, is it not?"

"But of course."
The dwarf agreed.
"That is the question.
Where does one find the real?
Within the heart?
Or outside the heart?
Tell me,
which brings more joy?
The winter's cold, for you?
Or, for me, the blossoming bouquet of snow flowers
given in love?"

"Yes—but where is the reality?" insisted the troll.

"Precisely," observed the dwarf.
"Precisely,"
and then said no more.

In the silence
both took note
that the autumn rain had ended.
The breeze was crisp and clear
as it swirled under the bridge,
and the dwarf bowed low,

> said "Thank you" to his host
> and smiled
> quietly to himself
> in joy,
>   a matter of the heart.

Group Ritual

The **Rite of Acceptance** formally marks the discovery that all which appears real is not necessarily real. What we see is not always what we get, and therein lie the seeds of faith. This suggested ritual and the accompanying variations are intended to assist folks in coming to appreciate that reality in the time surrounding the Rite of Acceptance. They are suggested here as a supplement to the rite.

At the gathering immediately preceding this one, invite the individuals to bring to this gathering some object which is special to them. At this gathering, then, each person shares that special object (the real) as well as the meaning (the really real) it holds for them. Photographs or letters should be discouraged since they in themselves implicitly represent something other than what they are. As each person shares their object, it might be placed in the center of the gathering to serve as a collective focus of meaning in everyone's life. This quasi-ritual could serve as a helpful context for some of the later questions or might even be used as an introduction to the story with the questions for discussion following the story.

Another development of this suggested ritual might be to incorporate the **Presentation of a Cross**, if the cross has not already been presented as part of the Rite of Acceptance. After all have explained their objects of special meaning and placed them in the center of the gathering, the leader may then give to each catechumen a cross—a call to live the contradictions of faith as well as being symbolic of what is truly real in life. If the catechumens have not yet been given a bible, this might be an alternative to the cross since the scriptures are an accounting of what the community has discovered to be the truly real.

Reflection

Reality is not always real. What we get is not always what we see, and so somewhere along life's line we learn to trust our hunches and listen to our inner voices. In some strange and inexplicable way, those subtle and quiet nudges are more often true than not. Reality is not always real; it is sometimes hidden behind the real.

When we were teenagers, our gang used to stand on street corners and stage arguments for passers-by—not fist fights, but shouting matches with a few appropriate shoves and pushes just to put the necessary exclamation points on the faked authenticity of the fight. Cars would slow, heads would turn, and we would laugh once they had passed—amazed at our newly acquired realization that illusion could be in our power and that reality need not always be real.

We do get good at such games, too good, so that for many of us we reach the point of being unable to sort the two—the real from the really real. When are our words truth and when are they posturing for a cry of "uncle" in one of life's tugs-of-war? When is love truly love and when is it no more than infatuation's slight-of-hand illusion? Black is not always black; white is not always white. And so we begin to look for someone to help us do the sorting. We begin to sense inexplicable longings for something "more" even though we find ourselves unable to explain what that "more" might be or how we might know when we come upon it. The gurus of pop-psychology we find fascinating for their insights into our own spirits and hearts. We keep our ears attuned for hints to recognize the real, and when it happens we sense we may have found a home, and we decide to stay there for a while just to see if the place is comfortable and warm.

Jesus, more than anyone else, was the master of such sorting, and perhaps that is why he had to be killed. He kept calling people's attention to the reality behind what they thought was real, and he insisted that that reality was the reign of God, the kingdom. Reality was not in being right but in forgiving, not in powerful control but in service, not in owning but in being free of the weight of such possessions, not in being loved but in loving. He had to be killed because if he was right, then the world as many saw it then and still do could indeed be a lie and all of life a masterful illusion, and such a realization would call for the dismantling of such a world—a process much too painful for many to imagine.

He *was* right, of course. The reign of God is not out there beyond Cloud 909 but rather among us, right here. Like fish in the sea and birds on the wind, we live in the very breath of God. Those who have eyes that *really* see, and those who have ears that *really* hear, do seek first the reign of God, and the illusion no longer deceives them, for life has become a matter of the heart.

Questions

- Do you remember at what point in your life you began to recognize a difference between the real and the really real?

- What do you treasure/appreciate/look for in people?

- Of all the different qualities of Jesus, which particular one would you hope to enflesh in your life?

- What is the tangible value or gift you have found in this particular community of faith?

Resonating Scriptures

- John 14:9-11 (To have seen me is to have seen the Father)

- Matthew 13:10-17 (Happy are your eyes because they see)

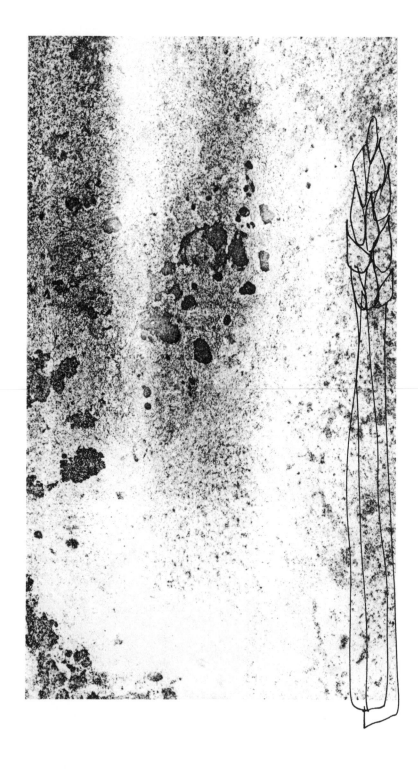

ASPARAGUS
FOR CHRISTMAS

IT WAS A DAY OR TWO BEFORE CHRISTMAS, as best I
can remember. The snow swirled haphazardly, tossed
back and forth among the bumping winds. And if
there were any carols being sung, they curled and
drifted and bounced against the grey December sky
like the smoke seeping from the tall chimney stacks
pillaring the horizon. That winter day was as fuzzy
then in its happening as it is now in its being
remembered. So I cannot promise that this story is
true in all its detailed brushmarks. Only the portrait
itself lingers in my memory.

My Aunt Agnes was coming to spend the Christmas
holidays with us, and I didn't like it—mainly because
I didn't like her. Uncle Bernard, her husband, had
died the week before Thanksgiving that year. My
mother had insisted then that Aunt Agnes come to be
with us for Thanksgiving, but Agnes had preferred to
stay home. She would be alone, she explained, but
she didn't mind; in fact she wanted it so. It would be

a time for paging through her book of memories, she had said. So we had Thanksgiving without Agnes, and no one seemed to really mind—especially me, though I never dared say it aloud. "After all, she is your aunt," my mother would have said, "and family needs to be family, especially during the holidays." And so it was, now at Christmas, that family would be family.

Agnes was to come by Greyhound bus a day or two early. I'm not really sure when. I only remember the swirling grey, as I have said, as well as the swirling spirit of Christmas which everyone else seemed to curse in its midst but love at its edges. For me, it was the best time of year, and Agnes was about to spoil it all.

I'm not really sure why I didn't like Agnes. Part of it, I know, was because she always wanted me to sit on her lap, even though I was already eight years old. She would pull me onto it so quickly that she always caught me off guard, and then when I would blush as she would hug me to her bosom, she would tease and ask what it was that made me turn so red. Of course I could never admit what it was, and she would always say it was so cute and made her want to do it all the more. That, I think, plus the fact that she would always ask me questions like "How's the third grade?" and "Are you and your brother getting along?" and then proceed to answer her own questions with her own personal stories—I think all of that put together, in addition to the fact that Agnes was like Agnes and no one else I had ever met, all made me, at least mentally, back away from her.

Without a doubt, in those weeks before Christmas that year, I had become quite obnoxious—though the why's of it all were and still are a part of the swirling grey. Certainly the impending prospect of Aunt Agnes contributed to the mood, but there had to have been more. It may have been my continual failures at mastering the "times tables"—especially the eights. Perhaps the fact that my best and only neighborhood friend had gotten the measles and then the mumps so that the only person to play with was my younger brother—a curse which by itself would have been enough to turn all of Christmas into a sack of coal. For all of those and perhaps many other reasons, my mother could barely cope with me and all of my antics. Her repertoire of usual disciplines depleted, she began resorting to threats of violence. "If you don't behave, we'll have asparagus for Christmas dinner" or "Your brother'll get all of your gifts" or "You'd better listen, young man, or your only Christmas gift is going to be a dress." Such outbursts on her part were not new and had never been carried out before, so the fear and obedience they were meant to instill never really blossomed. And yet, one had to be cautious.

The morning of the day Agnes came was spent in frantic cooking and vacuuming and laundering. Agnes seemed to have this hold over my mother to be the perfect housekeeper, and by virtue of family membership it was being passed on to us.

When the doorbell rang, my mother's last words to me on her way to the door were, "Remember, young man, you stay in line or it'll be a Christmas dress for you." Her words were so perfectly timed to prevent me from answering back that she completed her sentence and began her greeting of Agnes as she swung open the door without even a breath in between. It was odd, it seemed to me, that as the door swung open to Agnes so it also slammed shut upon the joy of the season.

Agnes' arrival came with a Christmas swirl of kisses
and hugs to her bosom. She patted each of us on the
head and asked me how third grade was and if I'd
been getting along with little Johnny. I tried my best
to be both proper and polite and even told her how
glad I was she'd come for Christmas (though
admittedly with fingers crossed behind my back). She
seemed pleased by my welcome and, with a hand on
each of my shoulders, leaned back to take a better
look at me, and then hugged me to her bosom again.
Oh, how I hated that.

Agnes came bearing gifts. Santa had come early to
her home, she told us, and so we could open these
gifts before Christmas, but most certainly after
dinner when all the dishes were washed and dried.
That afternoon seemed interminable as the kitchen
clock dragged the last few hours of daytime into the
evening darkness. In time my father came home from
work, and dinner was on the table. It was difficult to
remember our table manners and not gulp our food.
From my chair at the dinner table I could see the
boxes Agnes had brought piled in the living room—
treasures waiting to be unearthed. Both Johnny and
I volunteered to clear the table (a previously unheard
of event in our home) while we urged my mother to
hurry with her meal so she could begin the washing,
and Johnny and I finish with the drying.

The dishes finished, we finally gathered together
before the magical mountain of gifts. I remember
Johnny opened his first, though what his gift was
escapes me now. Being the next youngest, it came to
me to open mine. My mother always urged us not to
tear the wrappings, though why I was never sure
since it seemed she never used them again. However,
since the "real" Christmas was yet to come, I thought
it wise to cover all the bases of expected goodness,

and so I tried to be gentle with the wrappings and take my time opening the gift. With the paper off, I held before me my first gift of Christmas, ready to be opened and waiting to be cheered. I took a breath, lifted off the cover, peeled back the layers of tissue paper, and gasped. It looked like a dress—but it couldn't be. Yes, it was. I couldn't bear to lift it out of the box; then everyone would see. Yet it made little difference, for I knew everyone was waiting to know what I had received. Millions of thoughts raced through my head. How did Agnes know the threat? Had my mother told? Even if she had—why had I been given it? What had I done? Why did my mother betray me? Why from Agnes? How would I save face? Did I have to say "Thank you"? I couldn't. What did this mean? Was it a mistake? Had I done something unforgivable?

For a moment I sat paralyzed, kneeling on the floor. I looked up. Everyone was smiling, waiting for a reaction. Didn't they know? Were they so cruel? Then the tears. I pushed myself away from the gift, then turned and ran out of the living room to my bedroom and slammed the door. It was better to cry alone.

It took little time before both my mother and Aunt Agnes came knocking at the door of my room with tears and apologies. Aunt Agnes explained, at least four times, how in her rush to catch the Greyhound bus she had grabbed the wrong box from her closet shelf—as it turned out, a dress for a niece on the other side of the family. Over and over she insisted how badly she felt and how embarrassed by her mistake. My mother, on the other hand, kept saying how guilty she felt for trying to make me behave with such foolish threats and how terrible a mother she must be—if only I wouldn't be scarred for the rest of my life.

I, for my part, quickly came to understand how the mistake could have happened. More than anything, as I remember, it was their tears which convinced me, but also the fact that Agnes offered to take me downtown the very next day and buy me anything I wanted as her Christmas gift to me. "Anything," she kept saying. "You just name it."

With an eye on my mother, I said to Agnes, "Even a Wham-o slingshot?"—something I'd been hinting at since Thanksgiving but was not expecting, given my mother's answer every time I raised the possibility.

"Even a Wham-o sling shot!" said Agnes, even before my mother could object. It was then that I knew they were both truly sorry, for every year Agnes would give Johnny and me flannel pajamas for Christmas. A Wham-o sling shot was so out of character, it had to be something serious for them both to do something "against their better judgment."

The three of us dried our eyes, then, and together we went back into the living room. Absolutely no one said a word about the dress—ever again, not even my brother who could be merciless if he had something on you. Not even he. As we walked back into the room, I saw my father off in the corner wink at me and smile, as if he had heard the bedroom deal and wanted to say "Well done!" but couldn't. To this day he and I share that unspoken secret, a word enfleshed between us.

Reflection

I have been asked, "What would you like for Christmas?" so many times that I have grown no longer sure of how to answer or what to want. So in recent years, with a bit of tongue in cheek, I've said, "Oh, just some love and understanding, I think. That would be fine." I do think, however, that I have gone through life feeling fairly loved and for the most part generally understood, so I am not quite sure why I keep that answer on my gift list—unless, it dawned on me, that just maybe I don't feel as loved or understood as I think I am.

When someone really pushes me, however, on what I would *really* like for Christmas, and when I begin to take the search seriously, I come upon a list no one could ever begin to fill. There are moments of life that would make great gifts—like an evening with a longtime friend and a bottle of wine and a mellow fire and the sort of conversation that takes you into the wee hours of the morning without even a glance at your watch. Now that would make a great gift. Except no one can give such a gift. Oh, we can give a bottle of wine or someone can invite us over for an evening, but the real gift is just that, pure gift.

A new friend would also be a gift unsurpassed—if it were possible to give such a gift. Not that there is anything wrong with the old friends. Indeed, they grow better with age, like the old wine of memories or of common sense. Yet there is also something exciting about a new friend, about discovering once more the spirit which dismantles all the walls and barriers we have erected in self-defense only to realize they were never really as powerful as we had thought.

Another marvelous gift would be one of those occasional moments when Murphy's Law is not only suspended but seemingly superseded by some mystical law of benevolence and graciousness. I realize such grace when once in every thousand times I do choose the fastest line in the supermarket— when everyone in front of me pays cash, when no one needs a price check, and when the same checker stays at the same register for more than five customers and has all the change s/he needs. Now I don't really expect such gifts to happen, but I do keep hoping. And they do happen, occasionally—when my elbow knocks a glass of milk into wobbling across the table without spilling; when I am late and the bus is just as late and we meet at the corner in synchronized tardiness; when (if you have to get the flu) you get it on the night of the most boring social gathering of the year and are able to honestly call and say "I'm sorry, I can't come. I'm sick"; when you wanted to turn left but traffic forced you right and you unwittingly found yourself in the direction you wanted to go in the first place. Life is scattered with such graces, and if it were possible I would very much appreciate a book of such coupons entitling me to cash them in on moments of my choosing. Wouldn't that be a marvelous gift?

You see, there are moments when it does seem that life carries us and turns us into what we would have rather chosen had we thought of all the possibilities— except that *we* didn't and *God* did. And suddenly we find ourselves gifted with utter generosity, a whim of contradiction and delight—not so unlike the story of David and his sidekick prophet, Nathan, and their ever-confounding Lord God, Jahweh.

It was David who, after much turmoiled warring, had settled the people in their homeland and his own

family in a palace and then began having pangs of
guilt about God not having a home or temple for
Godself. So David, in a moment of daydreaming and
reverie, wonders aloud to Nathan that maybe he,
David, should build a house for God. And Nathan, in
good sidekick fashion, agrees. That night, however,
Nathan has second thoughts. Having changed out of
his prophet robes and into his prophet pajamas, he
sits on the edge of his bed talking over the day with
his God. Oh, not the way you and I talk over the day
across a cup of coffee or glass of wine. No, more like
you and I sitting on the edges of our beds and
thinking back upon the day and saying to ourselves,
"What I shoulda said was..."—that sort of talking
over with God. And there, snared among the
bouncing shadows of candlelight, Nathan comes to
realize that what he should have said was that there
was no need for *David* to build *God* a house because
God was going to build David a house, a royal lineage
to be known henceforth as The House of David. And
so Nathan blows out his candle and with it his
conversation with his God as well and rests so much
better because he knows what he will say to David
come morning—which is just what he does. There
then is when David has the tables turned on him and
finds himself pulled into one of those wishes of life he
would never have thought of choosing, which is what
God does mostly with our lives anyway—pure gift.

It is the story of a young Hebrew maiden as well,
making plans for marriage to her young beau, Josef,
and plans for a family and a future and a life lived
happily ever after, only to discover that *God* has
decided to make a life for *her*—a life she would never
have ever dreamed of or imagined, except that it did
come in some sort of angelic fashion daydreamed by

God out of what could be and into what is—
forevermore. Now that's a gift.

Questions

- Share a surprising "by-product gift" (some quality or characteristic or benefit) which came from a special relationship with family or a friend in your life.

- Has faith gifted you with such a "surprise"?

- Has God ever turned the tables on you, gifting you with the opposite of what you expected, only to have it all turn out all right?

Resonating Scriptures

- Luke 1:26-38 (Gabriel's Annunciation to Mary)

Group Ritual

The **Catechumenate** can be a time filled with discovering the surprises of God in one's life. It is a time to realize how faith is indeed a gift and a time for gratitude at having been gifted in such a way. "Asparagus for Christmas" can be a delightful interlude in the "business" of the journey simply to reflect on the gift of one's faith.

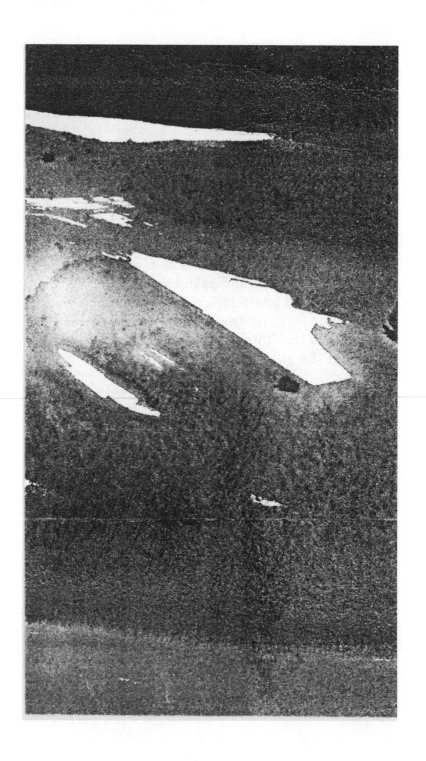

THE SHELF

AS DANIEL CRAWLED INTO BED THAT NIGHT, he knew
it would be a long night. He knew from the start he
would not be able to fall asleep. The next day was his
birthday—the ninth one. He had scattered many
hints about his conversations concerning what he
would like for a gift, and that certainly contributed to
the excitement he felt. But this birthday was
different. Daniel had been born on the ninth day of
the month as well as in the ninth year of the century.
Everyone had told him this was to be a special
birthday. Yet whenever Daniel asked what it was
which would make it special, no one seemed to know.
They only shrugged their shoulders and smiled in a
way which seemed a strange blend of knowing and
not knowing—and perhaps more of the latter.

Long after the house had been put to sleep, Daniel
was still wide awake. Restless, he slipped out of bed
and quietly floated past the door of his parents'
bedroom. He rode the banister down the stairs so the

steps would not creak and then groped his way through the dark downstairs to the back door. All of the bedrooms were in the front of the house. By going out the back door, there was less chance anyone would hear him leaving.

Barefoot and in his pajamas, he sat on the porch steps for a while, and then wished he had brought some shoes or worn his clothes. The distant wood, tucked in the clearing beyond his backyard, looked fun in the still moonlight. He knew that wood well and often spent time in its trees. It was a night when the summer coolness had not turned the darkness chilly, so Daniel decided to make his barefoot way to the familiar woods. The picket fence needed caution with his baggy pajamas and snagged his pajamas leg as he swung over, almost wrestling him to the ground. But Daniel recovered quickly. The drifting creek was easily crossed barefoot, and then it was an easy run to the edge of the wood, for the grass was long and smooth on bare feet.

Daniel stopped at the edge of the wood. It seemed darker and less inviting now than it had from his back porch. He glanced back toward the house; all was still quiet and dark. No one had heard him leave. But now that he was there at the edge of the wood, he almost wished they had. He would not have had to recognize his fear and could have forever lived with "if only."

He reminded himself that he knew the wood and all its paths, and that he was unable to sleep anyway. The moon was bright, and the wooded edge not very thick. The path was clear. So off he went, though to where he was not sure. Perhaps, he thought, he would climb his favorite tree and perch himself to watch the creeping moon turn the nighttime sky from east to west.

He found the tree without much fuss and swung up easily. He knew the holds and braces for his feet almost out of instinct, so many times had he climbed this tree. And from his perch he could see all around—his own house still dark and quiet, the creek he had crossed and its grassy field, and the neighbor's garden back- to-back with his father's. Here he felt safe and sure, as much as he had in his own bed.

But then Daniel saw a flicker of light. It caught the corner of his eye and came from behind some heavy trees to the right of where he sat. It did not move as though it might if someone were carrying a lantern. Nor was it a fire which burned bright and faded. It was steady and unmoving as if from someone's window. Yet Daniel knew the wood, he thought. It was not big, and never had he come upon a house within its bounds. Daniel moved to another part of the tree, and still the light shown strong, playing hide-and-go-seek through the branches of the trees.

By now Daniel had come to feel at home, and all the fear of when he had first come had seeped away. Daniel wondered whose home it could be. He wondered until common sense gave way to curiosity. Then he swung himself down from the branch on which he sat, let himself hang from that branch, and then dropped to the packed, dusty-smooth earth beneath. Quickly he brushed off his hands on the pajamas and began scouting a way to come upon the housed light without being seen—just in case he would decide he did not really want to be there and then could swiftly run for home.

Daniel stayed off the main path and, by way of his own shortcuts, worked a path toward the light he saw from his post in the tree. He ducked under a low branch, and as he came up he suddenly found himself before a tiny fieldstone cottage set in the middle of a small clearing. Daniel blinked once, then twice, and still the cottage was there. Now the wood seemed strange, different than before. He knew he had never been there before, but how that could be Daniel did not know for he had crissed and crossed the wood many a time and had never even seen the clearing, much less the cottage.

"Hello, Daniel!" The voice slipped out from behind the tree. "I've been waiting for you. This birthday is special, you know. I'm glad you found your way."

Daniel's heart roller-coastered through his chest as he spun around to see who spoke. There, behind the branch under which he had just ducked stood a tall and kindly looking old man—at least to eight-going-on-nine-year-old Daniel he looked tall and old. And kindly—well that is a judgment of the heart. "Who are you?" choked Daniel aloud.

"Dievas," came the answer. "I know you're scared. No need to be. I'm sorry if I frightened you. But I had to hide, or you would've stayed away if you had seen me. Would you like to come inside?"

Daniel followed Mr. Dievas inside the one-room stone cottage. It was simple and plain, furnished with a kind of peace. Daniel immediately felt at home— almost as if he had been there before. But he had not. He surely would have remembered. He would have remembered the jars.

The cottage was ribboned at eye level with a shelf, beginning at the door and going around the entire cottage, even along the wall made of glass, all the way around until the shelf came to a stop at the other side of the door. The shelf was narrow, as wide as the palm of his hand, and held only jars. Each jar was about three or four inches high with a cork stopper on top. All of them looked the same, identical except for the label on the front. Daniel looked at the dozens and dozens of jars, each holding something different. The first was marked *daydreams*, then *kisses*, another *magic*, and still another *answers*. The next, *problems*. Daniel slowly walked around the cottage reading all the labels as he made his way. *Storms, mornings, blessings, tears, wishes, pain, sun, laughter, peace, hopes, rain, fences, dreams, hurt, doors, death, sorrow, stones, promises, fears, smiles, pain, wisdom, keys, birth, clouds, rainbows, new life, joy, shadows, sparkles, dust,* and on and on and on. Daniel quit reading long before he came to the end. I would have remembered the jars, thought Daniel, yet it all seemed so familiar.

"Why do you have all these jars?" asked Daniel. Mr. Dievas simply smiled, his head bobbing the twinkle in his eye.

"It's your birthday," explained Mr. Dievas.

"You mean I can have one of the jars?" Daniel was growing excited now, having quickly forgotten both his mother's manners as well as the strangeness of the cottage which had brought him there.

"Well, almost," replied Mr. Dievas. "Almost. Allow me to explain. Tomorrow morning, Daniel, when you wake up, it'll be your birthday. You'll be nine years old. But it'll be a special birthday because you were born on the ninth day of the month in the ninth year of the century."

"But I don't understand," questioned Daniel. "Why does that make it special?"

"Though no one ever remembers—nor will you tomorrow morning, Daniel—it is special because of the choice you get to make. Whenever anyone's birthday matches the day of the month or the year of the century, they get to choose a gift for their lives from any one of these jars—twice in every lifetime. While whatever anyone chooses always comes to be, no one ever remembers having made the choice. Yet it's true, Daniel. We always become the kind of person we want to become. Always."

"But my birthday tomorrow will be a double birthday because the day of the month matches the year. Does that mean I can choose twice? It would only seem fair." Daniel began to sense that he was going to be treated differently than everyone else.

"We'll see," said Mr. Dievas. "We'll see."

Daniel began walking around the inside of the cottage a second time, only now more slowly than before, wondering, if he had to choose a jar, which it would be. "Why would anyone choose *tears* or *pain* or *storms?*" wondered Daniel outloud. "Why would they choose such unhappiness, Mr. Dievas? Why wouldn't they reach into *sun* or *laughter?* I bet no one ever takes the bad ones, do they Mr. Dievas? I bet those have been there for a long time, huh?"

"Well, to be honest, Daniel, those are the very ones most often taken, ones like *sorrow* or *hurt.*"

"But why?" Daniel insisted now. He felt he had to know.

"Oh, all sorts of reasons, I guess, Daniel," began the explanation. "Some take *sadness* because they feel guilty for something they've done. Others take it because they feel guilty that their life has been so good, and they see so much suffering in other people's lives. Somehow they want to even up the score, it seems. They never understand that all those other people had a choice too."

"Does anyone ever choose *death*?" asked Daniel.

"Sometimes," said Mr. Dievas. "Sometimes because they're tired of living. Other times because they're angry at someone they love who hurt them very much, and they want to get even with them. Everyone has his or her own reason, Daniel, and everyone's is different."

"Does anyone ever choose from one of the good jars?" It all seemed so confusing and so new for Daniel. He kept asking more and more questions.

"Sure they do," explained Mr. Dievas. "But usually they're younger children. They seem to be able to understand goodness and beauty as good and beautiful all by itself. It doesn't have to be a reward, not does anyone need to feel guilty about it. Little children see that more clearly, I guess."

Daniel chuckled to himself, "It looks like it's better to be born early in the month. Isn't it, Mr. Dievas?"

"Almost looks that way Daniel. Almost looks that way." Mr. Dievas nodded in agreement. "Most people seem to think someone else is responsible for their lives. Then when things go bad, they have someone to blame—God or the devil or bad luck. It's all a matter of choosing, Daniel. Nothing more. We always become the kind of people we want to become. We always do.

"Now—about you, Daniel. Tomorrow it's your birthday." Daniel sensed the moment of decision was almost upon him as Mr. Dievas continued to explain. "If you wish, you can choose any two jars you want, though I suspect you'd probably choose one from the happy side and one from the sad side. Most do who have the choice of two, though I must admit I think it's rather foolish that they do. But they do. Or, if you wish, Daniel, you can have one choice—the one from that unmarked jar in the center of the window."

Daniel had noticed the jar before, but had not paid much attention to it. Now his curiosity was eager. "What's in that one, Mr. Dievas? Why isn't it marked?"

"If I told you what it holds, Daniel, there'd be no need for it to be unmarked," explained Mr. Dievas. "But as it is, it takes much trust to choose the unmarked jar. If you choose from that one jar, Daniel, you'll be choosing to allow life to unfold as it will. Life will be good, trust me; though I must tell you now, it will not be without pain. But it will be good, and you won't regret the choice—though like everyone else, you won't remember having made the choice. But you will be at peace."

"But if I don't like it, Mr. Dievas, I won't be able to change it next time, because I won't be back again, will I?" Daniel saw clearly the implications of his choosing.

"That's right, Daniel. You won't be back again. That's the risk, and that's the trust. Only to those who have double birthdays as do you, do I explain the choice. Everyone who comes can choose the unmarked jar. It's always there. But only to people such as you do I explain it here since you come but once."

"Can I ask you one more question before I choose, Mr. Dievas?"

"Sure, Daniel. What would you like to know?"

"Have I ever been here before? I don't remember being here. Surely I'd remember the jars. But it all seems so familiar. Was I here?"

Mr. Dievas simply smiled. And then he shrugged his shoulders. "It's time to choose, Daniel. The time has come."

Daniel slowly made his way around the room one last time, reading all the labels and thinking of all that had just been said. He stopped, then, before the large window which looked out upon all of life, and before the jar without a label. He looked back over his shoulder at Mr. Dievas and smiled. Then he reached for the unmarked jar and held it, still sealed, in his hands. Only once, he thought. Never another chance. With his fingers Daniel pushed against the cork...

"...Daniel, Daniel, wake up. It's your birthday today." His mother's voice gently nudged him from his sleep. "Get up, sleepy head. You're nine years old today. It's a special day. I've made your favorite breakfast. Hurry on down."

Downstairs, Daniel pulled himself up to the kitchen table stacked with pancakes and sausages and all the fresh orange juice he could drink. What a great way to begin his birthday, he thought to himself. This was going to be one special day.

"Daniel," his mother asked with surprise as he began his second plateful of pancakes, "what happened to the pant leg on your pajamas? It looks torn and ripped." She bent over to look more closely. "And look at your feet. They're all dirty. Where were you? How did they ever get like that over night?"

Daniel thought it strange, for he had taken a bath before he went to bed the night before. And how it was that his pajamas leg was torn, he had no idea. For a moment he paused between forksfull of pancakes as if he had forgotten something, but then went on eating, unable to remember the dream.

"You know, Daniel," added his mother, "when I came down this morning the back door was wide open. Strange, because I thought I locked it last night before we went to bed. I guess I must not have." Daniel simply continued eating his birthday breakfast, trying to remember something he had forgotten.

Questions

- If you had to choose only one jar from the shelf, which would you choose? If two, which two?

- Do you believe that we always become the kind of person we want to become? Have you ever had that experience?

- What is it about the gospel that you find so appealing that you could choose to be a follower of the Lord Jesus?

- Why choose to live out your Christianity as a Catholic? In other words, what is it about Catholicism that moves you to choose this church community?

Reflection

In the Church of the 1950s, a teenage boy who thought of becoming a priest often went into the seminary after grade school, and while popular wisdom as well as practice have both come to new and different visions, the era of Pius XII bore its own kind of fruitfulness. I went to St. Lawrence Seminary as a sophomore in high school, and I went as a quiet and shy adolescent. It was in that first year, however, that the dynamics of a boarding school taught me how being somewhat obnoxious could lead to peer acceptance and recognition. There a hidden Joe, who even I had no inkling ever existed, came to the surface, the dynamics of a personality waiting to emerge with a breath of new wind. Since then I have often wondered whom I would have become had I made a different choice, had I gone to a regular high school. Would I have still discovered the boisterous flipside of a shy and quiet coin? Would different values have shown their face, and a different lifestyle been the norm? Would I have married? And become a parent? And lived in a small town instead of big? And been more involved in the community? Or less? Who would I now be?

Choices are indeed the seeds of our futures, and they sprout with all the excitement of anticipation—some to bear much fruit, some little, and some not at all. But even barrenness is a kind of future. Perhaps that is why choices generate so much passion, precisely because the future is there to be created and not simply to be accepted or watched in its unfolding or passively tolerated. Tomorrow will come whether we choose it or not, but the way it blossoms, well, that is another matter.

Popular belief systems would have us attest that our futures are issued along with our birth passports into life. Whom we will marry, where we will live, the number of our days, the rise and fall of our personal and collective "reichs" are all, it is thought, if not pre-planned at least pre-known—all as if we were living out a divinely previewed video.

Yet if we are indeed free, if our wills are not predetermined, can even God know what will be, since what will be does not yet exist? It may be that God knows all the possibilities. It may be that God knows all the probabilities and even all the likelihoods (given our own personal inclinations and predispositions). But might it not be that even God cannot know the future with certainty simply because the future does not yet exist—neither in our minds nor in God's mind, neither in our reality nor in God's?

Choices are indeed the brushstrokes with which we paint the portrait of our lives. So the Rite of Election is not merely one more stepping stone to becoming a Christian, but rather an integral piece in determining who we shall be—one who chooses to live in the image of Jesus.

Resonating Scriptures

- Deuteronomy 30:15-20 (I set before you life and death. Choose life.)

- Luke 18:18-35 (The rich young man who went away sad)

- Matthew 4:1-11 (The temptations in the desert)

Group Ritual

This story would certainly be appropriate for use as part of the **Rite of Election**. It reflects the choice the catechumens make at this point in their journey into the Christian faith community.

A possible alternative is to incorporate "The Shelf" into the **Rite of Acceptance**, or sometime immediately following that rite, in a way which would include the Presentation of the Bible. In this instance, at the gathering immediately preceding this one, ask all to prepare for this gathering by choosing in their prayer a gospel story which would stand as a name or title for their life. At this gathering, then, tell the story of "The Shelf," proclaim a scripture (perhaps Deuteronomy 30:15-20 would be appropriate), and invite each present to then share the fruit of their prayer by telling the gospel story which "labels" their life. As each one does so, the leader presents the catechumen with a bible—the believer's source of life. The prayer then closes in song.

Yet another possible use of the story would be to incorporate it into the **Presentation of the Lord's Prayer**, which is ordinarily found in the week following the Fifth Sunday of Lent. Having presented the Lord's Prayer to the catechumens, invite each person present to share which phrase of that prayer is an appropriate title or "label" for their life at this time. An alternative would be to share which phrase best names what they need from the Lord at this point in their life.

LIKE BATHING IN THE PHARPAR

AS CREATION WROTE HER POEMS
upon the cresting swells of blue-green sea,
Bahia Honda Key was most blessed
among all of the island keys
which dripped from the tip of her Florida pen.
Except for the sea grass, dried and brown,
only skittering sand-pipers and occasional pelicans
clutter her sandy rim and coral shores.
There the sun still rises without embarrassment
and nights are yet quietly guarded
by a blushing moon.

Once, on a day
when the clouds had beached themselves
upon the afternoon
and while the tide had left in search of other climes,
I met a bearded island dweller

peacefully adrift in the backyard of his world.
From the way he roamed that shore
this was obviously his home.
We nodded as we passed
and smiled,
sun enough to scatter the clouds.
An hour later we passed again,
each of us making our way home,
and smiled once more.
I told him, then,
he looked as if he lived there
and with another smile I apologized
for trespassing upon his stretch of home.
He laughed out loud,
kindly though,
and talked of when he'd come
and why he'd stayed
and how the island was not his,
but now he the island's.
Like the dweller himself
his story was homespun
and wise—
enough of both to make it memorable.
I came when I was young,
he told me then,
when few ever came to this lonesome place;
I came intending to stay only briefly,
at most a year or two—certainly no more.

In the home of my birth, he continued,
I had been told that true wisdom is found
only by journeying into one's heart,

and if I would wish to know the way
the shealtiel, the wise one in our land,
would know that way.
And so it was that I sought him out.
I asked him if he knew the way
and would he share with me the secret
of growing wise by journeying into one's heart.

He said he knew the way,
at least in part,
for his was a journey still not completed,
but one on which his own spirit yet trod.

I grew excited and eager
and asked him once more
if he would share with me the way,
but he only apologized
and said it was not his to tell;
besides, he added,
if he would tell me how
I would not believe it.

Oh, I would, I would,
I insisted,
if only he would entrust its path to me.

The shealtiel explained to me, then,
how he too had once sought for himself
the path into his heart,
but how part of the wisdom he had found
was that each had to find the way oneself.
If I wished to discover that path, he said,
I might find its beginning down at the sea.
If I would but live there,
the path would be shown.

I went home, then, and thought,
how foolish the advice the shealtiel had offered.

What would I learn at the sea, I thought,
that he himself could not teach me.
But then one day as I walked alone by the sea
I realized that if the shealtiel had asked me
to perform some extraordinary task
and to do something unusual,
if he had asked, for example,
that I bathe in the Pharpar,
the river which ribboned his mountain home,
I surely would have done so.
Why not then this which was so simple?

So I came here, then,
to this island shore
and lived here
alone
in quiet waiting.
The year or two I had originally intended
passed on by
and still, I thought, I had not begun
the journey into my heart.
I waited more
and more;
a full ten years turned by
before I'd decided the venture had failed.
I returned to my home,
the land where I'd entered the cycle of life,
and sought out once more the shealtiel,
hoping his life had not yet ripened to death.

Along the Pharpar, as before,
I found him again
at one with peace and with wisdom
only more so than before.
He asked how I'd been
and wondered of my journey
and the shores my spirit touched.

I told him, then, of the decade I'd spent
seeking the wisdom he'd promised
and the way of the journey
into one's heart;
and I recounted as well all the failure,
a path never found.

The shealtiel only listened and finally inquired
if the sea had taught anything,
if any truth had come clear
during the years on the shore.
When I agreed that there had been many truths,
but never the one for which I had come,
he asked if I would share
the sea's bounty which had been given.
I politely agreed.

I recounted of how, when I first came to this shore,
I built a home in which to live.
It took much energy and attention,
and in time I completed the task.
Shortly thereafter a tempest was unleashed
upon both this island and the home it held.
The rising tides that year pushed me back
farther and farther.
So the following spring I built another home,
more simple than before,
and far from the shore,
but in doing so I found myself too distant
from the sea and her rhythms.
So then I left that home
and found that I lived best
by the shore of the sea
without a home.
It was the sea which taught me the value of living
simply.

Often I roamed her shores
seeking shelled treasures cast upon her sands.
Seldom did I find what I sought.
Yet when I came without intent
and roamed simply and without care,
then I found many, though I left them there
for then I had no need.
Indeed, the sea taught me
that life is truly willing to give
but only to those who come also willing to give
and never to those
who come seeking to take without exchange.

I spent much time along this shore,
always listening and hoping to hear
the secret of journeying within
and finding one's heart,
but the roar of the sea and the crashing of her waves
obscured all the quiet.
I could not hear
until the sea taught me to enter into the tumult
and there I found silence to be the center.

There was much which the sea did teach,
I explained to the shealtiel,
yet the one quarry my spirit sought,
I never found—
how I might journey into my heart
and there find the gift which is wisdom.

Having told the shealtiel
all that I now shared with you,
the shealtiel only smiled—
strangely, yet warmly,
and then bowed low toward me
as if with reverence
and said no more.

There the tale did end
and the island drifter said no more as well,
but only smiled to me and went his way
as I did mine.
I called a "thank you" after he had passed,
more as an after-thought, it seemed,
and he but waved without turning back.
The tale had been told and another begun,
nothing more mattered,
so it is with journeys into the heart.

Questions

- Have you ever "gone along with something" you wanted to resist, only to find something good there? Share the tale.

- What did you come looking for? Have you found it? What are you *still* looking for?

- What piece of wisdom have you learned in the time spent as part of this RCIA process?

Reflection

The other day, Alex Thien's column of Milwaukee-ese and local wisdom outlined one of life's journeys for us readers. He observed that when we are ten years old, we think we can live forever. Then when we're twenty years old, we believe we can save the world. When we're thirty, we think we can at least save the company. When we're forty, we think we can save our children, and when we're fifty, maybe we can at least save our marriage. Finally by the time we're sixty, we come to the conclusion that maybe we should just save aluminum cans.

Most of us find ourselves smiling at that not just because it's clever but because it is perceptively true—our own truth. And so we don't smile too obviously, unless of course we're over sixty and know by then that it is everyone's journey from which none of us humanoids are exempt—now or ever.

The fact is that all of us go through life in search of how to make a difference, and all of our excursions into personal treasure hunting ultimately resolve themselves into that one everpresent quest—to make a difference. Our sexual escapades are most often forays in search of love—for to love and be loved, we believe, reveals to us our worth. So too our conquests of the twin peaks of power and wealth convince us (at least for a brief illusion) that we indeed do matter. And if we dare be honest, how many of our religious quests arise from that same urge—our wanting to be holy or people of prayer or those who know God? Might they not as well at least be mingled with a hue of longing for self-worth and recognition? It is what we seek.

So we make our way through life seeking what we're-not-always-sure, and every once in a while blushing as we discover ourselves standing naked before the world all the while thinking we had been clothed in a garment of noticeable beauty and worth—one more of life's fools robed in "The Emperor's New Clothes."

Sooner or later, if we take the time to live with some quiet, we find not only the answer but also our worth, and we find it within our selves. There we sort life's clutter from life's treasures, life's distractions from life's meaning, and the wisdom then comes clear. For people of faith, it is at the water's edge that we begin that journey within. It is at baptism, the beginning edge of faith, that we begin the sorting. And it takes a lifetime, at least for most of us. But then, isn't that the journey of our lives anyway?

Resonating Scriptures

- 2 Kings 5:1-15 (Naaman the Syrian in search of life)

- John 4:1-42 (The Samaritan Woman at the Well)

Group Ritual

The echoes of water heard in the story of the Samaritan Woman on the **Third Sunday of Lent** as well as in the celebration of the **Easter Vigil** make this story appropriate for either occasion. Both Lent and Easter are times for walking the shore of our interior journeys.

A large empty bowl and a pitcher of water is placed in the center of the gathering. The story is told. Some sharing ensues. Then each person pours some water into the bowl; as each does s/he shares a portion of his/her wisdom that s/he has found. After all have shared their wisdom, an appropriate scripture is proclaimed (perhaps the story of Jesus and the Woman at the Well). Then each person comes and dips a small cup into the water and drinks from that "water of wisdom." The water which remains can be saved to be a part of the baptismal water on Holy Saturday night.

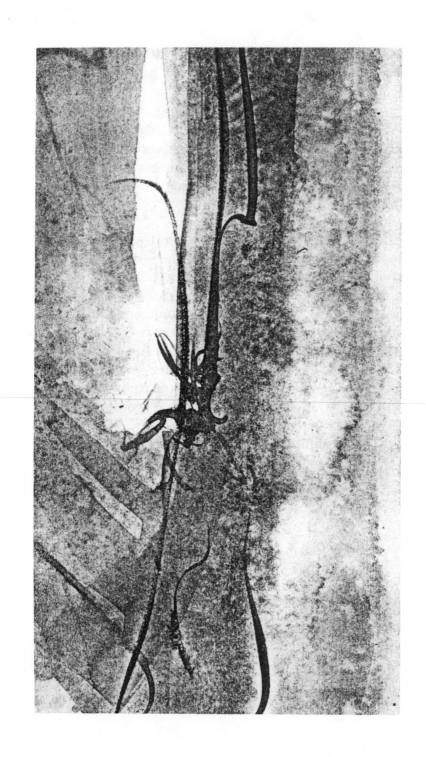

THE GULA

TREMBLING, he stood before the entrance to the cave,
a hatchet from his father's workshop in one hand and
a carving knife from his mother's kitchen in the
other. How he had hoped it would not come to this.
How he had begged his brother, six years his senior,
to share with him the secret, yet always his brother
had said he was not old enough. "Someday," he would
explain. "Someday. When you're older." Except the
day had never come. So now he would force fate's
hand and bring it about himself. No matter that he
himself had just turned six. No matter. He would
tackle the dreaded gula monster and come out the
victor just as his brother had before. The time had
come. His time.

Earlier he had weighed the pros and cons of
weaponry over hand-to-hand combat, of surprise
versus overt confrontation, of cautious entrance
against reckless charge. Now he quickly turned a
glance over each shoulder to make sure he was alone,

took one last breath for courage, and mumbled to his heart, "Gula monster, prepare to die."

Boldly he stormed the black fortress, flailing his weapons in careless abandon over his head and spewing curdling six-year-old screams against the black hollowed earth. No more than a dozen steps into the cavern, he slipped on the gula monster's slime and fell, sprawled in gravel and clay, weaponless from the jar of the fall. With the taste of damp dirt in his mouth and the pain of a bruised shoulder, he waited for the gula monster's growl and life-robbing claw to end the challenge. It never came.

After his heart had slowed a bit, he dared to open his eyes, just a crack at first, then wide to swallow all the darkness. The gula monster's den was dim and heavy with the dank smell of hidden life, but there was no gula monster. The cave was not big, smaller than his bedroom at home, and high enough for him to stand up straight and even stretch to reach the ceiling with his fingertips. The ceiling was cold and smooth with bumps, like he had imagined gula monster skin to be. Against the wall he made out a few old candle stubs laying in the dirt and a box of wooden matches, and he fumbled with them like all six year olds do whose mothers would never let them play with fire.

Once lit, the candles not only stole the mystery and the fear of the gula monster but also revealed the gathering place of his brother and his friends, the hideout every neighborhood gang of adolescents has. Once he saw the skeletons of their feasting, he began to understand—empty beer cans scattered about, the kind his father drank, he recognized, with orange sketchings on the label; cigarette butts crushed and flattened; and some magazines with pictures he had never seen before of women without their clothes on.

Slowly he put the pieces together, of how his brother wanted this place kept to himself, of how his brother had feigned his own battle with the gula monster with smudges of cigarette ash on his cheeks and self-inflicted scratches and bruises, of how the only gula monster that existed was the one created in his own imagination.

What the candles had destroyed was not only the neighborhood's sole gula monster but also his childhood. It was years later that he came to realize that most fully, but for the time being, in that slice of six-year-old life, he sat in the cave crying and not sure why, wishing he had never come in but not understanding that either. He thought of Santa Claus and the tooth fairy and other such friendlier gula monsters and began to wonder if they too were pieces of someone's imagination. He wished he hadn't seen the magazines and wondered why his brother kept them there. And he thought about trust and about believing older people and about whether something such as this would ever happen again in his life. Were there other gula monsters and other caves and other calls for wild and crazy courage? But most of all as he sat there in the cave he thought about how he did not want to go back out, of how life would never be the same again—*could* never be the same again. Something had died inside that cave, something besides the gula monster, and as he stepped back out into the day it was a different world, one he would have to learn anew as if for the first time.

Reflection

Despite what everyone says, I wonder if it may very
well be seeing and not hearing which is the final
sense and function which we surrender in death. Oh,
I do not mean seeing as in distinguishing between
night and day or far from near or polka dots over
stripes. No, that is a very different sort of seeing and
may very well be lost well before we die. What I
mean is the sort of seeing we do with our spirits, the
kind which reassembles the puzzle pieces of life in an
instant in such a way that we would hesitate to label
our life as our own—so radical then does our
understanding become as well as our perception of
what is.

On yesterday's local radio station the voice of the
rabbi observed that he had never heard a man on his
death bed wish he had spent more time at the office.
One's death bed does become a sorting field for all
life's energies and loves and deeds of fame. One sees
more clearly then—perhaps as never before. And the
rabbi made a point of noting that "the office" always
comes out the loser.

That is the type of seeing of which I speak—the sort
of seeing by which one understands more clearly
than ever before what the purpose of life is or what
one's world is about or what love truly is or, I suppose
in other contexts, what real evil is or sin or personal
greed or other such lures. Such revelations transform
in an instant the everyday humdrum of routine so
that we indeed wonder if perhaps in Nicodemean
fashion we were not born all over again into someone
else's world.

I suppose there are other instances too when such understandings come about slowly—as in over the course of a lifetime. The other day an old man and I passed on the path of a nature preserve. He moved along slowly, shifting back and forth between a shuffle and a stroll and scanning the wildlife along the way. "Sure are pretty flowers," he commented as we passed. I agreed with him and told him so, but that was all either of us said. To the two teenagers who had bicycled past moments before, the flowers were only weeds. But to him, and then to me because he had taught me so, they were indeed "pretty flowers"—wild sweet pea, tall and gangly thistle topped with whirling balls of purple, clumps of bouncing daisies, yellow I-don't-know-whats scattered here and there. What is that thread on which we string our years from childhood to adulthood to old-age wisdom? How is it that what is a bicycle path cut through a field of weeds for one is a rock garden of beauty for another? We do come to see differently in strange and unexpected ways.

Such is the seeing of faith, the coming to new vision, the stepping out of a cave and into sunlight so bright that the world can barely be recognized for what we thought it was. In the end, faith is not a way of looking at God. Rather it is discovering God's way of looking at life—all of it, weeds and flowers, success and failure, crying babies and crotchety oldsters, sumptuous banquets and day-old bread—all of it. It is discovering that we were all once born blind and that whether or not we see the weeds is not nearly as momentous as whether or not we come to see the flowers.

Questions

- Have there been life stages through which
  you have passed? Cave moments which have
  brought you to new ways of looking at life?
  Name one such moment.

- Some would say the movements from one
  stage to another are steps in maturity.
  Others would say they are part of the growth
  into holiness. If both are coming to see in a
  new way, is there a difference between
  maturity and holiness?

- Did you have a moment of conversion? A
  specific time you remember when you came
  to see with the eyes of faith? Was there a
  cost to that conversion? Something which
  you had to leave behind? A sadness?

Resonating Scriptures

- John 9:1-41 (Man born blind)

- John 11:1-45 (Raising of Lazarus)

Group Ritual

Seeing anew with the eyes of faith (the **Fourth
Sunday of Lent**) is not unlike the experience of
being called out of death and into life (the **Fifth
Sunday of Lent**). That experience puts one on the
threshold of a new creation. The suggested prayer
here attempts to ritualize that experience.

All gather together outside the church doors, either
in the open air or in the vestibule inside. Keep the
doors between those gathered and the church proper
closed. Tell the story. Share some of the suggested
reflection. Proclaim the scriptures. Then in formal,
symbolic fashion, open the church doors. All stand in

silence gazing into the new world awaiting their participation. Use a few minutes of silence to quietly reflect on the meaning of that new world. Close with an appropriate song (either listened to or joined by all)—perhaps something as "The First Song of Isaiah" or "Only in God" or some hymn capturing the mood of the gathering. All disperse from the entrance without ever having entered the church proper.

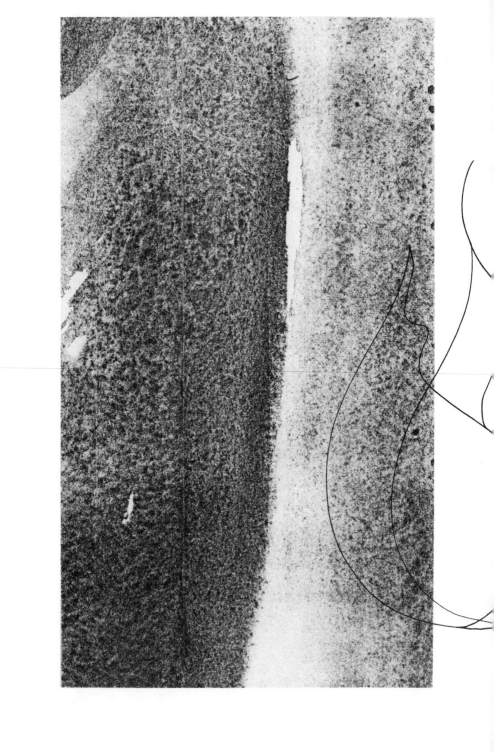

THE OIL BURNER

THE OIL BURNER IN THE LIVING ROOM had been
turned down to cool the nighttime. His wife of many
years had died; now, persuaded by his stepdaughter
to join her family in their upstairs flat, he sat alone
in the early morning gray. Yesterday had been the
moving day—but only of one suitcase and only of one
life. In the shadows of that shallow room, he
wondered how to read the ripples of those stirrings.

He had risen early, not from sleep but from his
wake-filled tossing, and come into the family's "other
room" to await the stirring of day. He had not
bothered to switch the light; there was not much to
see. He simply sat there, twisting the seamless band
on his finger, turning the hollow in his heart. When
the oil burner clicked and gushed with flame to heat
the day, his spirit stiffened, caught off guard by one
more new beginning.

It surprised him, too, when Nellie poked her head
into the doorway. He had not wanted to be caught in

such a mood. He had hoped his grieving to be private—no matter what others needed, then or now.

"You're up early," she said. "I didn't know you were such an early riser. Couldn't sleep?"

"No, guess not. Couldn't stay awake, either. Funny kind of living these days, I guess, without your mother. Sort of in between."

"Yea, I know what you mean."

He nodded to be polite. She didn't really, he thought, but how could he blame her? She only wanted to be kind.

She placed her hand on top of his, intending only to reassure him, and for an instant felt the ring and sensed then the emptiness she couldn't know, and thought her presence out of place. She scrambled some words about breakfast and such, then with a sleepy shuffle sought out her kitchen.

In the quiet, the oil burner clicked, and the gush of flame fell still. He wondered if the hollow echo of his loneliness would wake Nellie's husband.

Some fifteen minutes later, after the pools of darkness which had settled in their lives had been absorbed, only whispers of the grieving lingered about the conversation in the upper flat.

With her mother's death, Nellie's life had skipped a beat or two, but then quickly returned to its familiar rhythm. Her stepfather found peace, as well, though different than before. He smiled and teased little Joey as he always had, but with a different seasoning. She had worried about that for a while, then decided not to, for love reflected by a mirror is always twice as bright—so now, more dim, a face a bit more difficult to read.

Yet in spite of all her logic, Nellie thought she sensed his pulling back. Their gathering about the oil burner in the shadow of each morning had come to be a pattern, but now in recent weeks he had grown more quiet, or even absent from the day. She had begun to sense her need to find a balance for her love for him, ever teetering between interest and intrusion. Yet, the more she held her breath to hold the scales at level, the more he seemed to change the weights.

This morning she had found him there, beside the oil burner, more dressed than other days. "I think the time has come for me to move," he said straightforwardly—even before "Good morning." "Things will be better."

"I didn't know they were bad."

"Oh, I'm sorry. I didn't mean it that way. It's just that it's time. You're not really surprised, are you?"

"No, I guess not. It's just that I had come to be used to your being here, to our meeting here at the oil burner." She laughed at herself outloud, though quietly so as not to wake the morning. "Have you decided when?"

He paused to answer, answering her before the words did. "Today, I think."

"Why so soon? It doesn't need to be so rushed."

He only shrugged, then stood up and shrugged again. "I know. I know." Just then the oil burner clicked and gushed with flame, catching him off guard again as it always did. He smiled at the silliness of it all and placed a hand upon it, almost as if to bid good-by.

Nellie sat alone among the shadows, waiting for the morning light to sort the room, and wondered why he had pulled his hand away when she had reached to touch and reassure him. In the quiet, the oil burner clicked, and the gush of flame fell still.

Reflection

She not only wore her heart on her sleeve but her world too, and not only on her sleeve but on both sleeves and on her front and back as well. There she stood, next in line to receive Communion, to share in the Eucharist with the rest of that rag-tag community of believers, and I couldn't help but smile and wonder how she could be a magnet to all those buttons. The New Kids on the Block were obviously her nine-year-old world that day, for her denim jacket was barely visible through all the buttons of The New Kids she had pinned to her—top to bottom, front and back, shoulder to cuff of both sleeves.

The time will come, I am sure, when The New Kids on the Block will give way to other infatuations and other loves, and they will be worn as well—some bound with memories to the heartstrings of her youth and others banded in gold upon the fingers of her hand. Love gives a rhythm to our lives; it comes, it goes; it burns and fades in fickle indifference.

It is not only our love, however, which rises and falls like the tides, but also life itself and joys and dreams and even faith, all like the oil burner that heats our home. There is a rhythm that tugs at us, not only at our lives but also at our deaths, calling us out of those tombs where have found so much security.

In so many ways, we would choose to remain among the Lazarus shadows. We know full well that to walk out of the tomb only means that one day we will have to die again, for even Lazarus didn't live forever. It is almost as if life is never satisfied, a grass-is-always-greener caretaker slowly dragging us into death and insisting it is everyone's lot, yet also refusing to allow us to accept our deaths and remain in them but nudging us back into life. From doubt to faith to doubt again—and then again and yet again. From dreary loneliness to topsy-turvy trust in love and back into the frustration of love, the cycle cycles. From failure to success to failure. From sin to mercy to sin repeated only to be challenged by the offer of mercy once more. What is this force? Who is this love that will not leave us die in peace?

Questions

- Has your faith changed over the years? How? Why? Has it been painful?

- Do you have different faith questions now than you once had? Why do you suppose that is?

- Can you name some faith doubts with which you live?

Resonating Scriptures

- John 11:1-45 (Raising of Lazarus)

- John 12:44-47 (I came to be light to the world)

- 1 Corinthians 15:1-4 (The gospel will save you)

Group Ritual

The story and the accompanying questions/ritual/ scripture are appropriate for the **Fifth Sunday of Lent**. Because the ritual focuses upon the Creed, it could also be used in connection with the **Presentation of the Creed**, which takes place during the Third Week of Lent.

Those who have gathered together read the Nicene Creed in unison. The leader then reflects that we all live in the midst of faith rhythms, sometimes strong in our convictions and sometimes doubting or wondering where the truth does lie. The leader then invites individuals to share a phrase of the Creed about which each still has some sorting to do. After each has done so, each individual then signs his/her name to a copy of the Creed positioned in the center of the gathering. The signing is not a statement of certitude but a commitment to the search for truth in faith. A reading from scripture, praying the Lord's Prayer, or joining in song might be some conclusions to the ritual/prayer.

THE SITTING-ROCK

I TRULY WISH that the story I am about to share with you were of my own making. It is not. I first came upon it in a tiny wisp of creation in western Wisconsin known as Durward's Glen. Since I first came to know the story, I have come upon other people who also were told the same story, in the same place, and in the same way. So if it is your wish to verify its truth, all you need do is journey to the glen and listen with silence.

The glen was once owned by Bernard Durward, a poet, painter, and professor, as his tombstone perched on the crest of the glen attests. He lived in the latter years of the nineteenth century and apparently had acquired some local fame as a *literateur*. The glen affords an excellent opportunity for reflective escape, which is no doubt why Bernard Durward chose to spend large portions of his life there.

The glen is a small, cool canyon buttressed among western Wisconsin's rolling hills. A clear, spring-fed creek bounces through the glen, playing hide-and-go-seek first with the sky, then with the sandstone walls of the glen, and then again with the sky. The predominant texture and mood of the canyoned glen is green, for nature has mossed the huge boulders, hung ferns from the sky, and provided a massive awning of trees. If one discovers the glen, one also wonders if it is ever possible to rediscover the outside world.

In the middle of the glen, on the eastern edge of the creek, there is a large flat sitting-rock about a foot above the surface of the creek. It cannot be missed, should you go seeking it, for it is the only sitting-rock there so close to the water. It was there that I heard this story. I sat there in silence, my legs crossed and my eyes sealed by arrows of sunlight shot through the leafy sky. For a long time only the creek spoke with gurgly sounds, laughing at a world she had just eluded. Then, mixed with the song of the creek, the story began.

I am the spirit of Durward's Glen—not a ghost, you must understand, but a spirit. Giorgi first came here in the youthful years of his manhood and sat on the rock where you now sit. He came with dreams in his heart. As he sat on the rock with his eyes closed and his ears attuned to the glen, the spirit of the glen nudged his heart and there whispered a promise— three wishes you may have for whatever it is you dream, one on this day, the second ten years from now to the day, and the third ten years following the second. The only condition is that you return on the day of the tenth year following each wish. Giorgi agreed and here on this rock made his first

wish—sufficient wealth that he should never be in
need.

Giorgi left the glen that day and within the week
discovered he could purchase the glen and its
surrounding woods and fields if he but agreed to
settle and live there. This Giorgi did, building a small
hut near the glen and a waterwheel and mill
adjacent to the creek. The topsoil was rich, and the
crops of grain bore a plentiful harvest. Settlers that
followed also prospered on the land and brought their
grain to Giorgi's mill. In the ten years that followed
Giorgi's first visit to the glen, he became the most
prosperous of all the farmers in the area, both as a
result of his own fields and as a result of the income
from the mill.

Ten years to the day, Giorgi returned to the
sitting-rock along the eastern edge of the creek in the
glen. As he had done ten years earlier, he closed his
eyes and attuned his ears to the glen, and again the
spirit of the glen nudged his heart and whispered the
promise of three wishes. Giorgi expressed his delight
that his first wish had been fulfilled and hesitatingly
inquired if it were now possible to make the second of
his three wishes. The spirit agreed and there, on that
same sitting-rock, Giorgi wished for a family—a
loving wife and healthy children with whom he might
share his wealth.

Giorgi returned to his farmhouse and mill that day
with new hope that his second wish might be
fulfilled. Within that first year Giorgi met Marya.
They fell in love, and before the year ended they
exchanged vows. Soon children came, first a son,
then two daughters, and by the end of the second
decade a second son was born, enlarging Giorgi's
family to six in number. All were healthy, and their

beauty reflected the love of their dark-skinned father and their gentle-featured mother.

At the end of that second decade, to the day, Giorgi slipped back to the glen, alone, for he had never shared with his family the promise of the sitting-rock and the spirit's three wishes. For the third time in his life, Giorgi came to the sitting-rock, closed his eyes, and attuned his ears to the whispers of the glen. For the third time, the spirit of the glen nudged his heart and whispered the promise of the three wishes—this time with the gentle reminder that part of the bargain was to return at the end of each decade, even the last. To this Giorgi agreed readily, though he did not understand why it was necessary. The spirit only reminded him of the terms originally made twenty years previously and then inquired as to what Giorgi's third wish might be. To grow in wisdom among his fellows was Giorgi's third request. The spirit only smiled, as if to know the outcome and what would follow.

Giorgi returned, then, to his mill and fields and to the love of his family. In the decade that followed, he grew more and more prosperous as more and more settlers came to farm the local area's rich earth. In this decade, too, a third son was born to him and Marya. But most noticeable of all was how Giorgi grew in wisdom and in respect among the local inhabitants. While he milled their grain, they would pour out their woes and their struggles. Always Giorgi would listen and in the end would offer suggestions for healing troubled marriages and mending neighborhood conflicts. By the end of the decade he was known throughout the region for his wisdom and sense of justice. The third wish had been granted. Yet Giorgi could not understand why it was necessary to return to the glen—unless, he wondered, it was because he had been so generous with what he had received that now the spirit of the glen would grant him a fourth wish. So taken by this possibility was Giorgi that, even before the day of return had arrived, Giorgi had decided what the extra wish would be—one which could never be denied.

The day finally arrived and for the fourth time Giorgi returned to the glen. He walked straight to the sitting-rock, closed his eyes and attuned his ears to the whisper of the glen. The spirit of the glen was immediately present—as though it had arrived this time before Giorgi and was now found waiting. Giorgi immediately took the initiative and told how he did not understand the necessity of his returning a fourth time and how he had begun to wonder if it might not be possible for him to be granted a fourth wish—since the spirit and he were there together anyway. The spirit of the glen quickly protested, but Giorgi persisted and finally proclaimed that his fourth wish was to become holy. Could it be granted?

With that request, the sounds of the glen abruptly stilled. For a moment all motion ceased, all except for the spirit who quietly smiled as if it had been playing out a script written three decades earlier, only to find it all now come true. Very well, agreed the spirit of the glen. Since that is your request, be it so. It is now granted. Giorgi left the glen that day, thinking he had won the world and salvation too.

That summer a drought began in western Wisconsin. Giorgi's fields as well as the fields of all those in the area lay barren and scorched. Harvests of grain were minimal as was also the work in the mill. The following summer was no different. The entire area suffered now; even Giorgi and his family began to feel the oppression. The winter that year came early and was severe. It was during that winter that Giorgi's and Marya's youngest son began to fail in health. None of the doctors knew why, and before the spring thaw, their youngest had died and been buried. The following summer and the three that succeeded completed the six-year drought—one of the most dreadful in Wisconsin's history. With barren fields and a dried-up creek, the mill grew rusty and fell into disrepair. No longer did the local residents come; no longer was Giorgi recognized as one with wisdom. All had forgotten. During the fifth summer of the drought, both of his daughters fell in love and married. When the drought persisted for the sixth summer, both daughters and their husbands and newborns, grandchildren for Giorgi and Marya, moved to the growing cities near Lake Michigan in search of industrial work. Their moves caused Giorgi and Marya great pain, for now only two sons remained at home—and how long that could continue was doubtful. After the drought, Giorgi was never able to recoup his financial losses. Marya was growing more and more arthritic and as a result more and more house-bound. It was after such a course of events that Giorgi was forced to sell the glen (some say to Bernard Durward) in order to find some comfort in the final days for himself and Marya. To Giorgi it all seemed a most strange and painful decade to follow upon a wish for holiness. Perhaps he had presumed too much in requesting a fourth wish. Had he not been free of all anxiety and strangely at peace, it would have seemed to him almost a punishment.

The date on the bill of sale for the glen was exactly forty years to the day after Giorgi had first come upon the sitting-rock and the spirit of the glen that had promised three wishes. Having signed the bill of sale, Giorgi made one final journey to the sitting-rock. He came and closed his eyes and attuned his ears to the glen, waiting for the spirit of the glen to nudge his heart. The spirit did come and both sat in silence. Finally Giorgi asked why the fourth wish had not been fulfilled. Had he been too bold in requesting it? Had he failed in some way to be faithful? Why had he not grown holy?

To the contrary, the spirit began, the wish had been granted and fulfilled. To be holy, one must empty oneself of all of that to which one clings in life—of wealth, of knowledge and power, yes, even of possessing those who are the closest. Once one has emptied oneself of all that fills life, only then is there room for God, for even God cannot fill what is already full. Giorgi had begun the process of growing holy.

Thus the story ended. My eyes opened and I looked about. Nothing in the glen had changed—only I. The spirit of the glen had moved on; now only God's spirit remained, waiting to fill a life that first needed to be emptied.

Reflection

Every love story inevitably comes to a sad ending. At
worst, the love dies. At best, the love lives but the
lover dies. No matter how old, no matter how young,
that is the best one might hope for. Life does have a
way of stripping us of all we hold onto—even of love,
so that in the end we die empty, born into death just
as we were once born into life.

There is an old, proud oak outside my window. It has
stood there reigning for more years, I suspect, than I
have gathered in my own tenure upon this earth. It
keeps on growing year after year, broader and taller
and more imposing. The older it grows, it seems, so
also the stronger—a curious contradiction to human
aging. Noticeable of oaks, however, is how the leaves
and the trees remain bonded in deathly clutching and
grasping, even into winter, even beyond and into the
springtime of life's new cycle. The majesty and
beauty of the mighty oak grows cluttered with brown
and shriveled skeletons of last year's life. They are
indeed so much like ourselves—fearful of losing life
and so becoming wrapped in warped once-upon-a-
time beauty.

Life does take from us what we of ourselves would
never surrender, and that ultimate refusal to be
emptied may very well be life's only true ugliness.
The retired athlete who can live only in yesterday's
glory; the middle-aged adult who still dresses and
acts in adolescent guise; the parent who cannot set
his/her grown child free from parental moorings; the
person lashed to their hurt by bonds of revenge; the
long-endured marriage still snarled in mutual
combat for power and domination—all human beauty
turned ugly.

Like the barren tree carved in silhouette fashion against a winter snowscape, the emptied life takes on unimagined beauty against a backdrop of God. What is so magnificent about it all is that we need not choose it. It will choose us, each of us, in every lifetime. We need not seek it. It will find us. All we need to do is say "yes" in Christic fashion and watch death turn into resurrection.

Questions

- Share a time that you felt emptied. Did God seem closer or more distant at such a time? What emptiness do you need God to fill today?

- What is it in your life that you need to let go of, to be emptied of?

Resonating Scriptures

- Philippians 2:6-11 (Your attitude must be Christ's)

- Luke 23:44-49; 24:1-6 (Into your hands I commit my spirit)

- John 12:23-28 (Unless the grain of wheat dies...)

Group Ritual

The story is undoubtedly reflective of **Palm Sunday** and the journey of Jesus into the emptiness of death. Yet this same awareness may well arise earlier in the faith journey, perhaps during the **Catechumenate** when individuals share their responses to the call of the gospel in their lives. The accompanying ritual could be utilized on either occasion.

Those who gather are seated about a large, empty punchbowl placed in the center. In front of each person is placed a glass of water. The story is told. Following discussion, those gathered are invited to share something of which they must empty themselves, something of which they must let go. As each does so, s/he pours the water from the glass into the bowl. After all have emptied their glasses, a scripture is shared. All sign themselves with the water from the bowl as an appropriate song is sung. Everyone is then given some wine or grapejuice, poured into the same glass that once held the water, to taste the newness of the Lord that fills their lives.

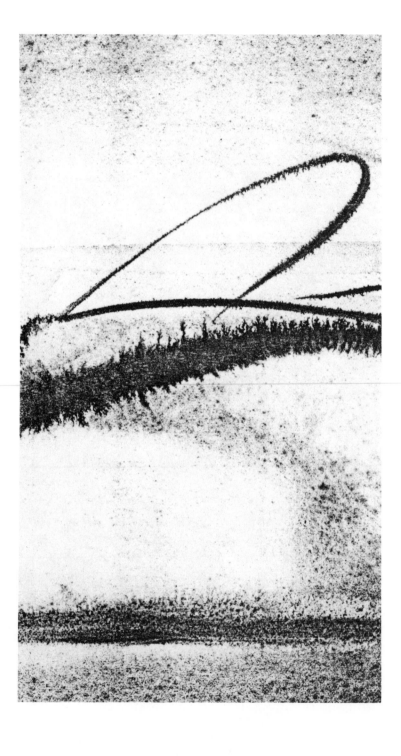

THE BOTTOM SIDE OF THE PUDDLE

IT WAS JUST A PUDDLE, much like most other
puddles, I would guess, except that this puddle was
up high, at least for an eight year old. Most puddles
gather themselves in cupped hollows as if they are
hiding or cringing from some intruder, in ditches or
along the dragging edge of a sidewalk or in mushy
grass at the bottom of a rain pipe. Seldom are
puddles up high.

I had just turned to the front side of being eight and
had come for a visit with my grandparents to spend
an entire week with them by myself for the first time.
They lived among some knobby hills out in what was
once country but had more recently become almost
city. There was a woods behind their house, not so
big that you couldn't see through it, but big enough to
fool yourself into thinking you could get lost in an
eight-year-old nighttime. Off at the corner of that
woods was one of those knobby hills, the sort you
could easily miss, yet high enough for the lone

chestnut tree at the top to float its crown above all the others and be seen doing so from the window in the bedroom I had been given. I'd go there to the top of that hill when I had nothing else to do, and I'd just sit under that chestnut and daydream the clouds and wish my life away in ways my mother always told me not to. Over the summers I came to spend at my grandparents', that hilltop became my "most favoritist" place in all the world. There are still times, when life gets rutted and mushy, that I dream of going back.

It was on that hilltop, under that chestnut, that I first came to notice the puddle. At first I hadn't paid much attention to it. I'd toss clumps of hard dirt into it or chestnuts off the tree, the way all boys and even some girls I've known do when they find a puddle all their own. And, as I said, I hadn't paid much attention to it until I came to realize it hadn't rained in days (or even weeks, my grandpa later told me). So I found a stick and tried to stir the bottom, except I couldn't feel the bottom, not even when I pushed my arm down into it. It was a puddle without a bottom!

That night I decided to ask my grandfather about it, or rather about puddles just in general, for I wasn't sure what-all was taking place. After we had finished supper and my grandmother had shooed me out of the kitchen, winking as she told me how she never let anyone help with the dishes, and after my grandfather had finished the paper and had moved on out to the front porch swing, I sat down next to him and waited on the silence.

"Grandpa?" I finally asked.

"Uh huh?" he wanted to know.

"Grandpa, how deep are puddles?"

"Oh, I guess it all depends," he said. "Depends on how big they are and on how much water there is." Then he didn't say anymore, until I was about to ask again, and then he almost quickly added, "Depends, too, on who lives there."

"On who lives there?" I asked with much surprise.

"Yup!" he said, then added an even bigger surprise. "Sounds to me like you must have found the puddle on top o' the hill beneath the chestnut tree. Only puddle around these parts that I know of that doesn't have a bottom—least, not one I ever found."

"So who lives there? I never heard of anyone living in a puddle, grandpa."

"Well, don't really know for sure. Long time ago, when I was growing up, the older kids always told us it was a Nighttime Monster who lived in the hollow inside the hill and would come out only at nighttime—hence it's name. We never believed those older kids, though, 'cause they always hung out in those woods at night, talking and smoking and doing whatever it is that older kids always do.

"Old Mrs. Peas used to live just the other side of that hill when we were kids. Her house burned down just after I got out of high school. Well, she used to say the Specter of Death lived in that puddle, but we always just sort of figured she said that to scare us from hanging out in those woods and making a lot of noise for her.

"I asked my own grandpa once, about the time that I was your age. He just looked at me and nodded a

smile through his pipe smoke and never said a word.
And I never asked him anymore either."

"So who do you think lives there, grandpa?" Now I
had to know.

"Don't really know, Joey, to be honest. Guess I hadn't
thought about it in a long time. But I remember
thinking once when I was much older that what I
should've done, back when I needed to know who
lived in that puddle, what I should've done was
sprinkled baking flour all around that puddle and
then come back in the morning to see if there were
any tracks in or out."

The swing came to a stop then, rather abruptly it
seemed, and so our conversation as well. The crickets'
chirp began to echo against our silence, and I excused
myself, saying I was going in to get a drink of water.
As the front screen slammed behind me, I could hear
the chirp of the porch swing begin again.

Grandma was just finishing the dishes and hanging
up the cloth with which she had dried them. "Can I
have a glass of water, grandma?" I asked, feeling a
breath of guilt about dirtying a glass and a kitchen
cleared of supper clutter. I gulped the water down
and caught my breath, then asked without a pause,
"Grandma, do you have some flour I could borrow?"

"Borrow means you're going to give it back," the
teacher in her showed its face. "You sure you're going
to do that?"

"Naw," I said. "I guess I meant if I could just have
some—for free. You got some, grandma?"

"What are you going to do with flour, Joey?" she asked, a foot each in curiosity as well as discipline. "I bet you and your grandfather have been talking about that puddle without a bottom, haven't you? And how he was going to sprinkle baking flour 'round about it to see if there were any tracks in or out?" She was already reaching for the canister, so I knew the answer didn't matter much in terms of whether I agreed or not. So I did.

"What do you think, grandma?" I wondered as I unwittingly turned the table on her. "Who do you think lives in the puddle? You think it's true? Maybe a nighttime monster, or death like old Mrs. Peas used to say?"

"Oh, he told you that too, did he now. Well let me tell you, Joey, I don't think either of them are true. If I were you, you know what I would do?"

I could feel my eyes grow big as Christmas as I shook my head. "No, what grandma? What would you do?"

"Well, I would take a long piece of old washline rope," nodding to her kitchen junk drawer as she spoke, "and I'd tie a big rock to the end of it and toss it into the puddle to see how far down it would go. There's got to be a bottom to it somewhere, Joey, and not so terribly far down, I would suspect." She said it all with a smile and a wink as she handed me a paper sack half-filled with flour.

The summer sun hadn't turned the day to close as yet, so I scurried out the backdoor and yard toward the chestnut on the hill. My heart beat to the rhythm of living dangerously as I raced up the hill and through the shadows that had come to roost with the nighttime wood. There was just enough dusk lingering about the puddle for me to see what I was doing as I tossed handfuls of flour around the puddle shoreline. I felt like Old Man Winter playing tricks upon a summer sprite, turning July into a winter snowdust. After I was all finished, I escaped the clutches of the dark by running down the backside of the hill, then took the long way home, round about the now-blackened woods.

That night I fell asleep gazing out the window toward the chestnut on the hill, my imagination waging war against the real. When I awoke, I checked the morning and found the nighttime hadn't changed the 'scape of the chestnut or my imagination's fantasy. Grandma had breakfast waiting—some juice and cold cereal—so I poured extra milk on the cereal to make it more drinkable and easier to finish off. Then I grabbed the rope out of her kitchen junk drawer, just in case the flour hadn't worked, and tossed a "thanks" over my shoulder as I rushed out, knowing full well she understood the balance of my plan and day.

Except for the change of dress from night to day, the puddle looked no different than it had the eve before. The flour lay undisturbed and trackless, as virgin as the day which held it. I kicked at the flour just to prove the plan was foolproof and watched it puff and billow. If indeed the puddle was home for some denizen of the deep, it hadn't left or hadn't returned during any of that night's trappings.

Almost out of expectation and without hesitation, I unfurled the coil of washline I had filched from my grandmother's junk drawer and tied a fist-sized rock to the end of it, lashing it both ways, front to back and side to side. With a deep breath, as if it were my last chance for wisdom and fame, I lowered it into the puddle. Deeper and deeper the rock took the rope until I held its barren end, taut and stretched. Even grandma's plan had failed, her wisdom no better than my grandfather's. Deliberately I let it slip from my hand and into its depths as I sat back against the chestnut tree. Frustrated, I spat toward the puddle, a target for my anger.

What took place then turned my life upside down—or perhaps right side up. It was then that I saw a rock floating in the puddle. My rock, tied in washline, floating! With a stick I hooked it and pulled it toward me and lifted it from the puddle, and with it the washline, foot by foot, dangling from the rock, dangling into the murky depths of the puddle.

Later that day, tangled in the dusk and confusion of all that had gone before, I lay on my bed and gazed out toward the chestnut king on the hilly knoll outside my window, wondering about all that had taken place. Much later—years later—I came to realize that, if at all, the puddle had only hinted at its mystery, hinted at the only answer that unraveled any sense. Perhaps life *was* lived upside down and downside up. Perhaps what we think life is is really the bottom of life and what we think is the bottom is in reality the top of life—a reality which, given the opportunity to show itself, will float to the surface, if only because it is most real. For the most part, where we live life is amid the darkened depths of confusion, and every once in a while we float up to the bottom and find ourselves at the light of a new puddle.

Much has changed over the years since that time. Both of my grandparents died, and their house was sold a short time after. I haven't been back to that part of the state since. So I wonder if the woods is still there and if the chestnut tree on the knobby hill still stands. Most of all, as you might guess, I wonder about the puddle and if anyone else ever found it. And sometimes, strangely, I find myself wondering if it all ever really happened—but then, maybe that's all part of the bottom side of the puddle.

Questions

- If you like the story, why did you?

- Of what might the puddle be a symbol?

- Have you ever found yourself confused by what is real and what is illusory?

- How is this a resurrection story?

Reflection

Mirrors always reflect what they see and only what they see, but they also reverse the image. In other words, if I stand before a mirror and wave my right arm, the image in the mirror will also wave its arm, but it will be the left arm that is waving, not the right.

Reality becomes even more confusing in a house of mirrors. There too the image reverses the reality, but the image of the image is identical to what is real. That is when the difficulty begins and the reason we get lost. Which is real, the reflection of the image or the image itself? How does the real me differ from the reflection of my reflection? Then which is more real and which less real? Me? Or the reflection? Does the first reflection, reversing the real, become the real because it is reversed in the second reflection? And so on and so on...

There we stand, lost, bumping into what seems real only to discover it is nothing more than a reflection. Yet we wonder which is the real and which the reflection. Us? Or it? And we keep on bumping! Panicking! Lost! Until we stop, until we move slowly, cautiously, realizing that for those few moments all of life is backward, nothing can be presumed, all needs to be tested. What is left will most probably be right (perhaps), and to move forward we must step backward (maybe). Above all, never presume that anything is as it appears. Only then will we find our way out of the maze.

Like a house of mirrors, the gospels seem to reflect life in reverse. All of our efforts to hold onto life seem to strangle what we hold, while when we are willing to enter into the struggle of letting go and dying, suddenly it seems we have more life than we are able to hold onto. Likewise, insecurity brings the peace which comes with having to trust in God, while the security we build with our own resources seems to be shrouded in the fear and turmoil of losing the very peace we supposedly have attained. When we grasp at sex in pursuit of love, love somehow eludes us, yet love given freely seems to enhance sex and transform it into love. Doing what we want in an attempt to be free enslaves us, while doing what our hearts insist *must* be done sets us free. Like the mirrors, the gospels reverse all that life says is true.

I watched some friends play backgammon not so long ago. I had always thought the game to be little more than a variation of checkers, more chance than skill, more a passing of time than thoughtful maneuvering. They rolled their eyes when I told them so and laughed to one another. Then one of them, the more masterful of the two, explained the levels of skill needed for the game and how one has to unlearn all the principles of the existing level in order to move onto the next level. What is true becomes false and what seems false is revealed as true. As in the house of mirrors, reality is continually reversed. Like the gospels, contradictions bear fruit. Like existence, life does not end in death. Rather, death ends in life. So in the real world, rocks float.

Only when we move slowly, never presuming that our way is God's, only then will we clumsily make our way out of this maze called life and into resurrection. From our perspective only this can be certain: that nothing can be certain, except our hope which is resurrection.

Resonating Scriptures

- Isaiah 55:6-9 (My ways are not your ways says Yahweh)

- Luke 24:1-12 (Why look for the living among the dead?)

- Matthew 5:38-48 (You have learned...but I say to you...)

Group Ritual

While this story harmonizes with the celebration of the **Easter Vigil**, that celebration is ritual *par excellence*. Thus, if the story is not used as part of the Easter Vigil, the following ritual might be incorporated into the **Mystagogia**, a time to reflect on the meaning of the most recent past.

At the center of the gathering, arrange a transparent bowl filled with water and, next to it, an assortment of pebbles, enough for each person to have at least one. Tell the story and follow up with some reflection from the suggested questions. Invite those gathered to drop a pebble into the water and, as they do so, to share a time when some hope or expectation turned to failure but in the end happened for the better (perhaps a relationship or business venture or eagerly awaited event or personal goal). After all who wish to share such an occurrence have done so, proclaim an appropriate resurrection scripture. Then close with the singing of a well-known resurrection song or hymn. As the song is being sung, all who have gathered come to the bowl and sign themselves with the water.

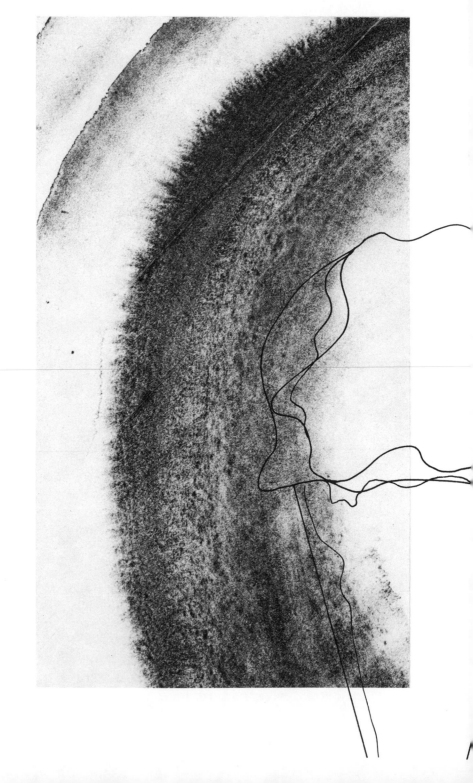

THE
ICE CREAM MAN

THE DAY THE ICE CREAM MAN CAME for the first time, he came as a stranger, ringing a bell and pushing his cart and giving away ice cream to anyone who came. The townfolk were not sure what to make of this newcomer scattering corner parties as he made his way through the neighborhoods. Yet he was the first shoot of happiness following a winter heavy with ice-bound darkness. So, while the children, excited and enchanted, skipped after him, the grownups simply watched from a distance, cautious and curious, yet jealously wishing they too could share the innocence.

One of the women townfolk did step out, away from the wall of adult gazes, to ask the ice cream man who he was and where he had come from. But the ice cream man only shrugged and smiled, kindly enough, she thought, and offered her an ice cream cone. How could she refuse, she wondered, and then found herself, ice cream cone in hand, being reeled back into her adult gathering. Once back within the wall, she felt as if she had betrayed a trust—though unsure whether it had been the grownups', who now watched her lick the luscious ice cream, or whether it had been the ice cream man's, who had stirred within her the new life of springtime.

Everyday thereafter, the ice cream man returned to ribbon his way through that little town. It was only on the first day, however, that he gave away the ice cream. On all the following days, the children of the townfolk came, clutching coins, exchanging treasure for treasure. And the grownups came as well, at least those not working in the fields or shops. Housewives and mothers gathered, and the retired folks came early, chatting and sharing memories already worn in their telling.

Before long, the townfolk found themselves looking forward to the sound of the ice cream man's bell and the clickety-clack of his cart. His coming came to be seen as a bit of a party in the midst of every day. Even among those who could not be there, the awareness that those they loved were able to share a bit of simple joy was a gift in itself. Day after day the ice cream man slowly transformed a winter people into new life, slowly healing the scars left by the biting cold and the searing wind.

Then one day the ice cream man announced that the next day would be his last, and that the last should mirror the first. A party of free ice cream for all the townfolk would mark the day, he solemnly proclaimed. Yet instead of scooping corner parties from his cart, he explained, there would be one large gathering in the town square. There the townfolk would officially seal their journey made out of the season of winter and into the season of summer growth—the fiftieth and final day of springtime partying.

On that fiftieth day, all the townfolk gathered in the square. All morning long, they continued to come till finally, by noon, all had arrived. Yet the ice cream man was not there. Into the afternoon they waited, and still the party had not begun. Some began to grumble, while others insisted that the ice cream man would not break his promise.

Then in late afternoon, the grocer in that town stood up before the people. For whatever reason, she began, they would never know why the ice cream man had not come. But perhaps his greatest gift, she continued, was not the party but the path from death into life which the ice cream man had revealed. "It's a path we need to celebrate," she explained, "so we don't hang on to our memories of winter and its death. Otherwise we might decide to stay there. It seems the ice cream man has shown us how to find each other. It's almost as if he gave us a new path—a path to one another. Now look—together we've become a new people. We've finished the journey. We need to celebrate!"

With that, the grocer invited those gathered to her store. There she brought out ice cream for everyone—enough till all had their fill. They sang and they danced, and together they celebrated the gift of fifty parties. When darkness came, they built a fire in the center of the square. Around the fire they settled, and in the tired quiet they listened to the stories of the ice cream man and his gift of fifty days.

In time, the children fell asleep, and then some others as well. The fire also tired till only embers glowed. Those few who still were not asleep said later that in the quiet distance they heard a bell—not unlike the first.

In the years that followed, the people partied each year for fifty days. Sometimes it was with much celebration but more often with quiet and with smiles. Always it was with ice cream and the ringing of a bell.

Questions

- Have you ever found yourself inheriting another's task once they were no longer present? What was it like to do so? Good experience or not?

- What are the experiences of your childhood which you would hope to pass on so that others might experience them as well? What are the experiences of this *RCIA* process you would hope could be experienced by others?

- How has your RCIA experience been like an ice cream party?

Reflection

John F. Kennedy made it sound exciting and momentous when he told his country that the torch had been passed—passed on to a new era and a new generation. The truth is that when one is carrying the torch, one can readily be burned. Once those gathered have dispersed, once the rhetoric is but an echo and the energy but a puddle left after the storm, then the one standing alone, torch in hand, has no star to guide him/her because, for the moment, there is nothing brighter—and that can sear us with blinding fright.

I remember years back standing at my uncle's coffin and realizing for the first time that there were no other living generations before me. Mine was the next, the oldest, the only one responsible. There was no other to blame. Only ours. Only mine. The baton had been passed, and though the symphony continued to play without missing a note, the need for new spirit left a rhythm of silence. Torches burn with different light at different times.

In the end, only a vacuum assures new breath, and so it was the parting of Jesus which set his Spirit free, free that we might do for others what he had first done for us. That indeed is what makes it so frightening—the expectation, or perhaps the realization, that together we must be the torched light that he was. That is also what makes it bearable and possible—that it is *his* Spirit still that burns in us. Not ours, but his.

That sense of responsibility may very well be one of the signs of the Spirit's presence in human life. No matter that different folks give it different names. No matter that it takes a different shape at different times in our lives. No matter that some are not even aware it is the Spirit. The conclusion which flows from such a sense of responsibility is always the same—all things coming together for the good of all.

It happens in becoming a parent: folks drive more cautiously, their selfish yearnings get whittled away, their extravagant consumption gives way to simple living for the sake of another—life comes together for the common good. It comes guised as promotion: the teacher becomes the principal, the laborer is asked to be foreman, the volunteer agrees to coordinate the service—life comes together for the common good. It comes about when people of faith share their faith with another, if for no other reason than because in some unexplained fashion, they find themselves moved to say to another, "I believe"—life comes together for the common good. It takes place in millions of instances when people say "yes" instead of "no" and love blossoms.

The torch was passed not only to John Kennedy. It is passed to each of us, every day, consciously or not. Accept it! Celebrate it! Have a dish of ice cream!

Resonating Scriptures

- Acts 1:4-11 (Ascension of the Lord)

- Acts 2:1-7 (Pentecost)

- 1 Corinthians 12:3-7, 12-13 (The Spirit given for the common good)

Group Ritual

One almost hesitates to suggest the obvious—a
Mystagogical ice cream party.

WIND AT THE CENTER

HE COULD NOT REMEMBER ever having not known the story. The tale had been part of his being a boy. He had grown up with it, set out into life with it, and now had begun to grow old with it. Whether or not it was even true, he had not been sure. Yet he had given his life over to the story and its quest, and now that he knew and understood, he wondered if that had been wise.

When he was young, Jonathan had been told how in the beginning good and evil had battled with one another. Then goodness did not yet know she was more powerful than evil, so she feared that should she lose in battle, all her wisdom which God had planted deep within her would die as well. Thus one night in the stillness of a quiet moon, she whispered to the wind all the wisdom she had come to know. And ever since that night, the wind has borne that wisdom, carrying it from age to age and people to people. Yet for whatever reason, it seems that few have ever heard the wisdom spoken by the wind.

When he was young, Jonathan spent much time listening to the wind. Yet he only heard what everyone else heard, never any more than the sound of life rushing to be born. Occasionally, before his childhood had run out, he had asked those who were thought to have wisdom how they had been able to hear what it was which the wind whispered. They only smiled at Jonathan, first at his innocence and then later, it seemed to Jonathan, at his foolishness. So by the time all of Jonathan's childhood had unraveled, he had learned not to ask the question.

Jonathan's occasional questioning, however, had not gone unnoticed. Vayas, old and forgotten by most in the village, had marked for himself those rare times when Jonathan had sought a way to find wisdom. So when the day came for the young lad to be knighted and formally bestowed with adulthood, Vayas took him aside. "Sir Jonathan of Conroy," he addressed him, "today you have been knighted in service of the king. For many years I've taken note of how you have longed to grow wise. No one has taken you seriously, and many have only smiled at your youthful idealism. However, if you wish, Jonathan, I can conclude for you the story of the battle between good and evil and where it is that wisdom can be found."

Jonathan blushed. He had not known he was being watched so closely. Yet he also was thrilled. What he had longed for could actually come to be real.

Vayas then finished the story begun so many years before. "After the spirit of goodness had whispered to the wind all of the wisdom she had come to know, she began to realize that no one might ever hear the gift,

for the wind always speaks in hushed and silent
ways. It was then that the spirit of goodness built a
castle marking the place where she and the wind had
shared the gift. There in that castle and at its center
was a room. Find that castle," concluded Vayas to
Jonathan, "and sit in the center of that room, and you
shall hear the wisdom borne by the wind."

So Jonathan set out in search of that castle. He
trudged the northern tundra, seeking a castle of ice.
He roamed the shifting deserts, scanning hot
horizons for a lone sandcastle. He visited the mighty
castles of the northland and told his story in the
strange-shaped castles of the East. Indeed, Jonathan
spent a lifetime of years in search of that one castle
with the room at its center where one could hear the
voice of the spirit. The only fruit of his efforts,
however, was much disappointment.

Weary and aged, Jonathan made his way home one
final time. He had endured all sorts of frustrations.
He had lived with pain and befriended loneliness. He
had suffered as well as rejoiced, spent days with the
poor and also with the wealthy, experienced both the
emptiness of success and richness of failure. Now,
only a matter of days from home, he had resigned
himself to ending his life without having found the
castle.

That day's travels ended in darkness, and Jonathan
found shelter beneath a tree along the wayside path
he had been following. With the new sun, Jonathan
awoke and saw in the clearing before him a small
castle, well cared for and bold in structure and shape.
Jonathan stood amazed and in awe before the castle.
He had seen many castles in his wanderings, but
never one like this. He walked around it, twenty
paces to a side, and scanned the walls, each a plum

line to the noonday sun. Strangely, there were no
turrets for battle, no drawbridge for security—oddly,
not even a door. Rather, its only entrance was a
tunnel beginning ten paces outside the wall and
leading beneath the wall and into the center of the
castle. Jonathan entered the tunnel and cautiously
made his way in the almost total darkness of the
buried passage. When Jonathan emerged inside the
castle, he found himself in a small but well-lit room.
It was round and carved from stone with four
corridors leading from the room in the four directions
of the universe. At the end of each short corridor was
a window, each sealed with a patterned grillwork
identical to the others.

Without hesitation, Jonathan recalled the story told
him by Vayas of a castle with a room at the center,
where one can hear the wind speak its wisdom and
truth. Whether it is the shape of the walls, Vayas had
told him, or the pattern of the bars on the windows,
whether it is the pitch of the ceiling or the texture of
the stone, or whether simply one place in all of
creation was meant to be the heart of wisdom, no one
knows. Nevertheless, if one sits in the center of that
room, one hears the wisdom of the wind as it blows
through the room.

The small room was bare of any furniture except for a
small round stool carved from stone at its center.
With anxious awe, Jonathan sat upon it. Had anyone
else been present with Jonathan, they would have
stood in amazement. All day long he sat motionless
and transfixed, until the setting sun began to seal
the windows in shadows. Then Jonathan stood up
and immediately left the room and the castle, almost
as if with urgency and purpose.

The following morning, Jonathan awoke beneath the same tree under which he had gone to rest two nights before. To his surprise, the clearing was empty and open. The castle of the morning before was no longer there, if indeed it had ever been there. Had the previous day been only a dream? Jonathan could not help but wonder. Yet why, Jonathan thought, did he now seem to understand life so much more fully than only a short time ago?

Jonathan sat in the morning's twilight, wondering and unsure. Finally, he stood up and walked into the empty clearing. What was he to make of the strange memory of the day before? He stopped at a corner of the clearing and parted the grass with a brush of his foot. There, before him, hidden by the growing grass, were two what-seemed-to-be paths at right angles to one another. Were they really paths, or perhaps the remnants of some foundation? He shook his head, as if to free himself of such thoughts. Still, he measured off the distances—four sides, twenty paces to a side, identical to the measurements of the castle. Then, ten paces off one side, he found a mound—the entrance of the tunnel, he wondered? But too strange to be believed. Yet it was all there, and life did seem to fit more clearly as well. Or was it only that he had finally lived enough to be able to piece it together?

Reflection

You and I live in an addicted society, which can only
mean that all of us are one way or another affected
by the disease and most probably are addicted
ourselves. Should someone ask us to name such an
addiction in our society, we most readily think of
alcohol or chemical drugs. Should they ask us to
name yet another, then food or gambling or perhaps
sex might come to mind. Gerald G. May, in his book
Addiction and Grace, names 183 addictions of which
he recognizes and admits to 14 in his life. Included on
May's list are such recognizable addictions as
chocolate and television and sports and cleanliness,
but he goes on to include some less-recognizable ones
as gossiping and intimacy and humor and images of
God. It seems we humans live with a hunger, and
most probably with more than one.

A while back, a high school freshman was telling me
of the new CD player he had just bought and of how
he had been saving up for it for what seemed like a
prison sentence worth of odd jobs. I smiled at his
"pain" and told him he sounded as if he wasn't sure it
was worth it all. Hands in his pockets, he shrugged
and said he thought it was—but then added a
lonesome tag. "You know what I was thinking
about?" he said, not quite sure of it himself, it
seemed. "After I bought that CD player, I started
thinking about what I wanted to save for next, and
suddenly I began to wonder if my whole life was
going to be just that—working to save to buy and
then just starting it all over again and never really
satisfied and always looking for the next best thing.
And I was sort of wondering if I wanted to spend my
whole life just doing that. And it all seems a little bit

of a waste to me—except that's what everybody else is doing. And still, I don't know. I really would like all those things."

What does someone do with a hunger that will not go away?

What someone does, what we all do, is try to satisfy the hunger—and maybe that's the way it was meant to be, which is not to say we should go out and wallow in a mud-puddle of fantasies. Yet the fact of the matter is, with permission or without, we human beings are experimenters. Whether it is acceptable or not, we all "try on" life with varying degrees of enthusiasm. It is the only way most of us can come to know how it is that so much of it in the end comes to nothing. For most of us, the only way beyond the illusion is through the illusion, until the only alternative is what people of faith call God. In other words, we need the hunger to taste God.

In some ways, Pentecost is the culmination of a story of hungers—people dragged (by the Spirit, perhaps?) through a banquet of life's entrees, through dreams of success and conquering victory, through visions of fame and adulation, through hopes for the future, through efforts at security and power and recognition, only to discover that they could never satisfy, could never do anything but leave one hungry, could do nothing but fail. Pentecost comes, then as the recognition that the hunger is Spirit herself threading us through all of life's temptations so that eventually we might come to know the Lord.

Questions

- Have you ever had a hunger satisfied? Have you ever searched for and found a deepest longing fulfilled?

- Do you have a wisdom place? A room at the center of your world where you go to find quiet and, hopefully, wisdom? Describe it and why it is important to you and how you came to have such a place or time?

- What piece of wisdom do you need at this point in your life? How will you know if you become wise?

Resonating Scriptures

- Isaiah 55:1-3a (Come all you who are thirsty)

- Romans 8:22-27 (All creation groans)

- John 7:37-38 (Come to the Lord for living water)

Group Ritual

The themes of this story and of the story "Like Bathing in the Pharpar" both have **Pentecost** in common. Thus the ritual suggested at the end of "Bathing" is equally suitable here if you have not utilized it already.

An alternative is to post a "Graffiti Wall," a posterboard or long piece of bulletin board paper. Invite everyone to write "on the wall" a piece of wisdom they have heard on the RCIA journey. If this gathering comes at the end of the **Mystagogia** with some sort of social evening or meal, the invitation to write one's wisdom should come early in the gathering, allowing everyone the time to note their wisdom whenever the Spirit reminds them. Finally, before everyone leaves, gather everyone in front of the Graffiti Wall to read it and celebrate it. Close with a favorite song or sign of peace. You might also consider posting the Graffiti Wall in a place benefiting the entire parish or saving it for a future group of journeyers.

Appendix

Story	RCIA Season	Theme	Resonating Scriptures
Bread That Remembers	Precatechumenate	Telling One's Story	Jn 6:46-51 (Bread of Life) Jn 16:12-13 (The Spirit guides) Jn 21:24-25 (More Jesus stories)
Chrysanthemums	Precatechumenate	God speaks through ordinary life	Gen 1:1-5 (God spoke; creation happened) Is 55:10-11 (God's word does not fail) Jn 1:1-5,14 (The Word became flesh)
A Matter of the Heart	Rite of Acceptance Presentation of Cross	What is real?	Jn 14:9-11 (Seeing me is seeing the Father) Mt 13:10-17 (Happy are eyes that see)
Asparagus for Christmas	Catechumenate	God's surprises	Lk 1:26-38 (Annunciation)
The Shelf	Rite of Acceptance Rite of Election Presentation of Lord's Prayer	Choices	Deut 30:15-20 (Choose life; choose death) Mt 4:1-11 (Temptation in the desert) Lk 18:18-35 (Rich young man)
Like Bathing in the Pharpar	Third Sunday of Lent Easter Vigil	Seeking wisdom	2 Kings 5:1-15 (Healing Naaman's leprosy) Jn 4:1-42 (Samaritan woman)
The Gula	Fourth Sunday of Lent Fifth Sunday of Lent	Seeing anew	Jn 9:1-41 (Man born blind) Jn 11:1-45 (Raising of Lazarus)

Story	Liturgical Occasion	Theme	Readings
The Oil Burner	Fifth Sunday of Lent / Presentation of Creed	Life rhythms	Jn 11:1-45 (Raising of Lazarus) / Jn 12:44-47 (Light to the world) / 1 Cor 15:1-4 (The gospel will save)
The Sitting-Rock	Palm Sunday / Catechumenate	Emptying	Lk 23:44-49; 24:1-6 (Into your hands) / Jn 12:23-28 (Like wheat that dies…) / Phil 2:6-11 (Christ's attitude)
The Bottom Side of the Puddle	Easter Vigil / Mystagogia	Reversals	Is 55:6-9 (God's ways, our ways) / Mt 5:38-48 (You've heard, but I say…) / Lk 24:1-12 (Resurrection event)
The Ice Cream Man	Mystagogia / Pentecost	Service	Acts 1:4-11 (Ascension) / Acts 2:1-7 (Pentecost) / 1 Cor 12:3-7,12-13 (Gifts of the Spirit)
Wind at the Center	Pentecost / Mystagogia	Spirit hungers	Is 55:1-3a (Come to the Lord) / Jn 7:37-38 (Jesus is living water) / Rom 8:22-27 (Spirit births creation)

Other Stories for Faith-Sharing

STORIES TO INVITE FAITH-SHARING:
Experiencing the Lord through the Seasons

Mary McEntee McGill

Paper, $8.95, 128 pages, 5½" x 8½", ISBN 0-89390-230-6

These stories are for you to read for yourself, or to read with a group and see how they encourage others to share their stories. Each season includes five stories and Reflection and Faith-Sharing sections to experience each story and season more fully.

THE LIGHT IN THE LANTERN:
True Stories for Your Faith Journey

James L. Henderschedt

Paper, $8.95, 124 pages, 5½" x 8½", ISBN 0-89390-209-8

This collection, linked to the lectionary, goes beyond facts to the "truth" of your faith journey. Use them for personal reflection, homily preparation, or small-group work. "Dennis Meets St. Peter" will make you examine your understanding of heaven and hell, while "Can This Be Home?" will challenge you to wonder about the exiles in your midst.

BREAKTHROUGH:
Stories of Conversion

Andre Papineau

Paper, $7.95, 139 pages, 5½" x 8½", ISBN 0-89390-128-8

Here is an essential resource for adult catechumenate, Cursillo, and renewal programs. Following each section of stories are reflections — keyed to the lectionary — from a psychological point of view, which will help you help others through their personal conversions.